The Little Green Book of Revolution

We have the technology. The problem is the oligarchy.

~Generally dedicated to the people on the streets, dirt and concrete, for always knowing first. Specifically dedicated to the Y 12 Three; Megan Rice, Michael R. Walli and Gregory I. Boertje-Obed. The Y 12 Three committed one of the most provocative acts of civil disobedience in order to make people aware of nuclear experimentation's dangers.

The Y-12 Three walked into the Y-12 high security nuclear complex to symbolically deface a uranium storage building. They used baby bottles to paint the building with blood, hung banners and hammered off a chunk of brick. They were convicted and sentenced to twenty years in prison and held without bail before sentencing. The graceful symbolic act was done to demonstrate nuclear experimentation's war on the unborn and the insecure nature of it, including the 'high security' installation. Megan Rice reportedly smiled to the judge on sentencing. In a war world revolution turns swords into plowshares.

"Every moment it's (nuclear weaponry/experimentation) an imminent threat to the life of the planet, which is sacred." ~Megan Rice

"I believe we are all equally responsible to stop a known crime." ~Megan Rice, self-described citizen of the world.

Contents-

"When the Earth is sick, the animals will begin to disappear, when that happens, The Warriors of the Rainbow will come to save them." ~Attributed to Chief Seattle

"When the Earth is ravaged and the animals are dying, a new tribe of people shall come onto the Earth of many colors, creeds and classes and by their actions and deeds shall make the Earth green again. They shall be known as the warriors of the rainbow." ~Hopi prophecy

Disclaimer from The Streets:

   The Little Green Book of Revolution represents Earth Mother, it does not represent any institution whatsoever. We all need to walk out from underneath the gargoyle wings of institutions. A little green revolution is required in order to live sustainably and in tune with Earth Mother, instead of raging against her to the detriment of all things great and small. There is nothing violent about revolution. In fact a revolution is nowhere defined as violent, whereas the status quo is totally violent, martial and punitive at every level. Revolutions are subject to the violence of the status quo just like everything else on a day to day basis. And a revolution can only be revolutionary if it is nonviolent, hence the requirement for a little green revolution. A revolution is a turning point, a revolving change, a little green revolution would turn away from the typical controlling, corrupt, violent and polluting institutions, returning to live as Earth Mother's children.

Peaceful action is the most revolutionary of all actions in the war world. A little green revolution would be a return to simplicity, assisting Earth Mother do what she does, foster life, instead of warring on each other and causing strife. Humanity is polluting Earth Mother permanently for temporary fulfillment. A little green revolution would stop such ill behavior allowing for development and integration. A little green revolution would minimalize the release of poisons for profit, not allow systematic pollution by credit. A little green revolution would shift from a mechanical and mineralogical based society to an agricultural and permacultural one, in sync with the elements.

Humanity is eating Mother Earth up, emitting poisonous waste to the point we are toxic to all life and our own offspring. We leave only ruin and desolation in our day to day operations. The water is toxic, the land is bereft of nutrients, the air is tainted, we are a carcinogenic nightmare unto ourselves and all life, and we debate global warming.

The global warming debate has led to catastrophic pollution denial. Global warming is equated with global pollution and thus the debate takes us away from addressing the evident problem, the fact we are essentially crapping our cot. The fact is the planetary pollution we emit casually and daily is devastating as to alter the climate and must be addressed. Global warming is symptomatic of catastrophic global pollution and debating it distracts us from addressing local and global pollution and the environmental destruction and elemental consumption.

Global pollution is the result of a sick culture. We have polluted entirety and created such confounding pollutants that all life on the planet is now dependent on the wellbeing of the engineer at Fukushima and the four hundred some other nuclear power generation experiments in the world. We have polluted entirety to the point that it is difficult to estimate to what extent. Another subtle catastrophic symptom of our consumption sickness is global dimming. Particulate in the atmosphere spewed by burning petrolithic material and other soot actually causes global dimming and global cooling in conjunction with global warming, resulting in the concealment of the problem of global environmental destruction. The particles literally block the sunrays as the gasses prevent the atmosphere from releasing heat.

Another concealed problem, this one just below the surface, is methane trapped in the melting permafrost of the world, the release of which could significantly impact our environment and enhance the warming effect. Altered global temperatures could result in the ocean currents shifting, which could again magnify change further, resulting in a horrifying tipping point.

Global environmental destruction causes imbalance in ways we are aware of and in ways we mostly do not conceive. The environmental destruction results from the selfish culture of separation. We enclose ourselves off from each other, from Earth Mother and sometimes from own ourselves. The environmental problems requiring a little green revolution stem from the mind state of mankind, how we walled ourselves in and allowed institutions to effectively war on entirety, the culture of separation. We separated ourselves so much that we consider Earth Mother, the blood of her waters and organs of her soil, secondarily to profiting from her. The culture of separation has led to postmodernism. Postmodernism remains a wobbly understanding because it is so new a concept, but it concretely began when dilution of pollution became no longer possible. In the postmodern war world there is only further saturation and accumulation of manmade carcinogenic trash.

The shift toward postmodernism was progressed by planetary island-hopping behavior steered by oligarchical institutions, but we all bear some personal responsibility. The worst problems we manifest for ourselves are nuclear and petrolithic mining, refining and burning, but the problem stems from our minds, the worst problem is within. Instead of taking responsibility it seems most of us prefer to continue to yield to operations of the status quo, believing bureaucratic deliverers of authorized facts, instead of spiritual and instinctual respect for reality allowing the pristine to be turned into poisoned. The mind states of many are so separated that we eat genetically modified organisms grown with toxins designed to kill everything except the modified organism

7

designed to survive in the poison and believe it's nutritious because an institution said so.

"Humankind has not woven the web of life. We are but one thread within it. Whatever we do to the web, we do to ourselves. All things are bound together. All things connect." ~Chief Seattle

We have saturated entirety with toxins on a race to nowhere and now it's necessary to return to sustainability, to have a little green revolution, to heal Earth Mother. Practical sustainability is entirely possible and absolutely necessary as postmodernism continues. We have the technology. The problem is the oligarchy.

The American Indians lived in harmony with Turtle Island, the name for North America, for millennia. In fact indigenous people all over the world lived in cooperation with Earth Mother for millennia as opposed to institutions that set up shop on Turtle Island and annihilated purity in a century or two. Turtle Islanders did not island hop, they migrated and moreover fostered Earth Mother's potential, the opposite of what the institutionalized do today. A little green revolution to heal Earth Mother can be accomplished using original American exceptionalism, Native American Indian culture of caring for each other and building surroundings. The difference between indigenous and institutionalized individuals can be demonstrated using an old tale of one group of Dutch newcomers living among Americans.

One day the Europeans showed the Americans how to use a hoe for planting seeds. One American was astonished at all the work it took to make such a magnificent tool and then was equally astonished at how wonderfully it worked. It was a great tool, but he began laughing at himself using it. And soon everyone was laughing unable to specifically communicate why because of the language barrier.

Later the Europeans discussed the moment. They were proud to share the tool with the Americans and referred to the laughter as reasoning for their pride, as an indicator the American felt silly for having not thought of the simple tool before. The laughter was proof they were superior for having thought of the garden tool and developed ways to manufacture it and bring it to Turtle Island. The Americans too, later discussed the moment sitting in a circle. They noted all the energy it must have required to find the materials to make the tool and laughed at the Europeans for having made such a thing and brought it all the way here when planting-sticks plucked from a branch worked perfect. Then they all heartily laughed again at the real kicker, that the Europeans didn't see the expanse of permaculture they had fostered all around as opposed to the tiny plot of squash the hoe worked. Indigenous individuals integrate with entirety and open gardens, while the institutionalized fence in gardens for themselves. All Indian tribe names mean essentially the people of, for instance Hopi means the people of peace. Institutionalized individuals identify themselves with institutions as opposed to individuals, or the people.

"I see a time of Seven Generations when all the colors of mankind will gather under the Sacred Tree of Life and the whole Earth will become one circle again."
~Crazy Horse

On observing the institutionalized newcomers the Americans referred to them as being spiritually afflicted. In Northern California, where there was astounding abundance and the people knew only peace, it's said many elders died of fright on encountering the violent newcomers. There were probably many descriptions for the craze the Indians saw, but one that survived is Wendigo. The legendary Algonquin monster with long claws ruthlessly ate people and everything. Those infected by Wendigo proverbially and actually devour the life force of people, places and things with insatiable hunger.

A Wendigo is similar to the Hopi description of Two-hearts. Two-hearts is similar to twofaced, but goes beyond it. Two-hearts speak one way with you and another way about you, they'll say one thing and do another. Two-hearts masquerade as kind, when all the while they're holding people in binds. A real unhindered human leads self with the heart and the mind follows. Two-hearts allow the heart of another to control them, usually the empty heart of an institution. They then have to feed the second heart and are always hungry, like a Wendigo. We are living in a Wendigo world of Two-hearts.

Ten thousand years of agriculture/permaculture in unison with Earth Mother doesn't just happen. In fact it's said the Hopi founded their home in the harsh Arizona desert as part of a plan; in the harsh desert environment they would have to cooperate with each other and pray for rain just in order to grow adequate food, so there would be no time for anything discordant. All American Indian tribes have many stories about how conditions had to be just hard enough so they did not grow soft, weak, or abrasive, in order to maintain brotherhood and take care of Earth Mother.

The Anishinabe from the Great Lakes have a story about how the maple trees used to drip sweet sap. One day the chief couldn't find anyone and eventually saw all the people spent their day lying under maple trees eating syrup and growing fat. He prayed and god made it so that the syrup had to be boiled down and that a lot of it had to be gathered just to get a little thereby making everyone happier and more appreciative of the fruits of their labors. All American Indian philosophy relates the importance of working together.

Incidentally, many conform to political correctness and label indigenous Turtle Islanders as Native American. In fact, I'm basically Anglo and was born in the U.S.A. and therefore Native American, but I am not American Indian or American indigenous. There can be no political correctness in revolution, for it quells thinking, only the pursuit and expression of truth, the instigation of thinking.

I have gathered together stories and quotes from American Indian culture to explore the idea of rainbow warriors, a little green revolution and at least instigate thought. Many of the related indigenous ideas are debatable as far as their specific accuracy and source, but after centuries of gentrification we are lucky to be able to at least verify the surety of their sentiment.

Despite the diversity of American Indians they all understood the Rule of Seven Generations and through it foretold the Prophecy of the Seven Generations as a warning to the newcomers who dug up and cut down Earth Mother. The Rule of The Seven Generations is to consider the impact of one's actions seven generations into the future. For instance, when harvesting one would make certain that enough roots and flowers were left to ensure continuous plenty.

The complexity of nuclear experimentation is beyond the pale of postmodern human comprehension. It reveals, no matter how we would like to believe otherwise, the postmodern mind's overall inability to consider the unseen. Whether invisible because of ethereal origins or because it's nano-sized poison does not matter, collectively we tend to obfuscate the unseen. Nuclear experimentation also reveals our collective inability to conceptualize time, and to understand how long nuclear radiation lasts, how insistent karma is.

At one time, seeing the unseen and considering the future was valued. In fact, indigenous cultures across Turtle Island, A.K.A. North America, believed they would one day return home to the spirit world and they all considered the Seven Generations rule when implementing any procedure beginning with harvesting herbs. The people were so considerate of others as to make sure there would be enough herbs left seven generations from their harvest. The Turtle Islanders contemplated the unseen and the distant future.

Today we have been taken away from such comprehension. In order for institutions to implement the military industrial complex, the prison industrial complex, the pharmacological industrial complex, as hairs on Wendigo claws, our collective mind state had to be steered from the unseen. No one would allow nuclear experimentation if they could see the spiritual or ethereal, rather than just money, no one would allow nuclear experimentation if they knew the Seven Generations Rule.

The gold hungry newcomers had no such wise respect. They called Turtle Island 'The New World' partly to reinforce the idea that it was open for plunder, as if there were not people who had been there for generations, and also because it was so well taken care of. Louis and Clark famously crossed the continent and were surprised that they could harvest and find food on their continental journey so easily. It was because of the Rule and the implementation of integrative permaculture.

On seeing mining, forestry, needless slaughter of people and animals, American Indians predicted negative outcomes seven generations after the takeover of the entirety of Turtle Island. Collectively known as the Prophecy of the Seven Generations it's said birds would fall from the sky, the air would burn the eyes of men and fish would perish in undrinkable water.

"In our every deliberation, we must consider the impact of our decisions on the next seven generations." ~Iroquois Maxim

The prophecy foretells environmental destruction. Another related specific warning shared by many peoples from Chile to Alaska; digging up the guts of Earth Mother will unearth great tragedy. This warning came well before the petrolithic and nuclear eras which realized the most potent hazards of digging up the guts of Earth Mother. It was about seven generations ago that mining for gold and other 'precious' metals was the main illustrated danger. Such mining reinforced the crazed genocide of American Indians and today over half the rivers in the U.S.A. are toxic, many from mining and/or industrial activity from decades ago. Today massive and sudden animal deaths are typical, just like foretold and many other dire circumstances manifest. Today Louis and Clark wouldn't make it.

"If we dig precious things from the land we will perish." ~Hopi prophecy

"When all the trees have been cut down, when all the animals have been hunted, when all the waters are polluted, when all the air is unsafe to breathe, only then will you discover you cannot eat money." ~Cree Prophecy

A little green revolution could begin by being true to heart, revolving back to living in cooperation with Earth Mother instead of separating ourselves from her, from one another and from ourselves. The fact that people still argue about global warming reveals Two-hearted thinking. We, the collective, would rather ignore total environmental destruction than consider changing our culture of separation and overconsumption.

The global warming debate is moot, the temperature is not the only indicator of global pollution. But if record highs and record lows are taken into account, a steady rise in record highs and decrease in record lows is apparent and sharp the last fifty years. This global temperature rise directly correlates with the initiation of the global digging up and burning up of Earth Mother's guts. But the correlation of temperature rise and anthropogenic pollution may only be a coincidence, for the sake of argument perhaps the temperature rise is due to a solar cycle.

So, forget global warming. The debate has allowed the talking dead in the lame stream media to reason not changing our polluting, war mongering ways and politicians the likes of Al Gore to promote pollution by credit instead of changing our polluting, war mongering ways. The global warming debate halts the real discussion. What are we going to do about our carcinogenic lifestyle? They don't want to talk about that because they can't say the radioactive elements, petroleum products and toxic chemicals in our water are due to increased solar activity.

A little green revolution would go beyond global warming. It could be a psychological revolution, like a technological revolution, only we just change our collective thinking. Revolutions are always more nuanced than convention.

The convention today is war and pollution causing Earth Mother imbalances. A little green revolution would seek balance. The debate on global temperature halts the debate on what to do about the global oligarchical system which is right now destroying creation for profit, right now breaking the Rule of the Seven Generations. Cease the global warming debate and suddenly global environmental destruction is obvious evident.

"I am poor and naked, but I am the chief of the nation. We do not want riches, but we do want to train our children right. Riches would do us no good. We could not take them with us to the other world. We do not want riches. We want peace and love." ~Chief Red Cloud

Institutions present solutions to global environmental destruction based on relieving institutional burden, where individuals pay biologically and economically. A little green revolution would side with individuals and subdue institutions, the main causation of global environmental destruction to begin with.

A little green revolution would open land for agriculture or permaculture for example, as places to build to benefit individuals and Earth Mother, for localization. Green is not red, red is red. A little green revolution would limit institutional globalization and uplift indigenous, individual localization.

If you are supportive of institutions then you better not read this. Stop here. If you discard the idea of Two-hearts and The Seven Generations idea, then maybe this is not for you. If the sentiment, 'fuck war' irritates you because of foul language and not because we still struggle with war, then surely there is other reading material more appropriate to your refined sensitivities. If you support war or condone foul language, if you support the status quo reinforced by Demoncats and Republicons or whatever leftwing/rightwing paradigm you're under, then you are probably trained to be hateful of revolution and you might as well stop right here. If the sentiment inspires you because the foulness of war makes such expletives appropriate, then I hope you'll read on.

"You can't wake a person who is pretending to be asleep." ~Navajo proverb

 "We will be known forever by the tracks we leave." ~Dakota proverb

"When a man moves away from nature his heart becomes hard." ~Lakota proverb

"The environment isn't over here. The environment isn't over there. You are the environment." ~Chief Oren Lyons

   We live in a Wendigo war world, a place where force dominates and an insatiable appetite for stuff is considered a quality characteristic. The ravenous Wendigo with its penetrating claws endlessly digging can only be confronted with open hands and open heart. Wendigos want and only by sharing can they be defeated. You cannot fight a Wendigo, for it is made up of colorless evil, fighting it only feeds it. A rainbow is the opposite of colorless evil. A rainbow is made from clarity and also is a reflection of every color. A rainbow is symbolic for omnipotent grace in its clarity and its ability to reflect all seven colors. A rainbow represents no thing and all things at the same time. Diamonds share this quality of clarity and ability to reflect. A rainbow warrior is like a diamond rainbow, clear but reflecting all colors, opposite of unclear evil and colorlessness.

   In order to be a clear rainbow warrior one sheds two-heartedness and stops feeding the Wendigo, one stops choosing colors or institutional reflections. When one resides in one's own heart, without impulses to speak for, act on behalf of and feed a second institutional heart, one clears institutional mediation of the Wendigo world. A rainbow warrior is clear of any institution. And at the same time a rainbow warrior represents all colors, all individuals, all beings. Instead of a wielding a sword the rainbow warrior has a clear heart and open hands. Rainbow warriors have their hearts in the right place, as well as having their hearts placed right.

"When I was ten years of age I looked at the land and the rivers, the sky above, and the animals around me and could not fail to realize that they were made by some great power. I was so anxious to understand this power that I questioned the trees and the bushes. It seemed as though the flowers were staring at me, and I wanted to ask them "Who made you?" I looked at the moss-covered stones; some of them seemed to have the features of a man, but they could not answer me. Then I had a dream, and in my dream one of these small round stones appeared to me and told me that the maker of all was Wakan Tanka, and that in order to honor Him I must honor His works in nature. The stone said that by my search I had shown myself worthy of supernatural help. It said that if I were curing a sick person I might ask its assistance, and that all the forces of nature would help me work a cure." ~Tatanka-ohitika, Brave Buffalo

The American Indians lived in harmony with their environment for millennia however there was occasionally disharmony among the peoples of Turtle Island. Tribes battled each other variously, but never on the mass scale of European war. The term bury the hatchet comes from the Iroquois legend of the peacemaker who brought together the five nations under the pine tree of peace.

During a time when people became unthankful there was war in every village. A vicious cycle of war and revenge spun out of control to the point no one knew what the fight was about anymore. A child was born to a virgin and when he grew up he traveled to all the nations to convince them to unite in peace. After a time, he was able to bring the people together and convinced them to literally

16

bury their weapons under a white pine tree and symbolically bury their hatred and vengefulness. He also tied together arrows from each tribe to represent their unity as one. Rainbow warriors have to make peace so we can heal Earth Mother. Without forgiveness and unity there will be no peace, without peace, there will be no healing. The world is very much in a state where we have forgotten what we're fighting about, living vengefully, continuing on a downward spiral of revenge and war.

Rainbow warriors are clear, and of every color or vibration, but a successful revolution must be green. Certainly the green symbolism of integrative energy is ultra-important and of immediate necessity for revolution, but further a successful revolution has to be green in relation the heart chakra. If a revolution is not begun in, and does emanate from the heart, if not done as an act of love then, more than likely the revolution will fail. The heart chakra is green and is central among the seven chakras. Centrality is indicative of power, grace, love and equanimity.

"Grown men can learn from very little children for the hearts of the little children are pure. Therefore, the Great Spirit may show to them many things which older people miss." ~Black Elk

One common American Indian tradition was to always feed guests. This welcoming attitude was accompanied with a qualification; that they have their own gourd to eat from. It's a practical qualification and if the world followed this one simple rule, if we all traveled with our own gourd or container, we would not have oceans and rivers littered with plastic leftovers. If we shared more and traveled with our own cup we would not have plastic gyres in our oceans. Some of the world's worst problems could be solved by simply returning to indigenous understanding, original American exceptionalism, as opposed to institutionalized living.

Global institutions banned growing hemp, from which we could grow material that can be turned into plastics, not to mention food, clothing, shelter and fuel. Instead we use the leftovers from petrolithic mining and refining as a source for toxic plastics which pollute entirety. This is a case in point where if we integrate instead of celebrate oligarchy we would not be forced to drink carcinogens.

The Time of NWO

NWO is the commonly recognized abbreviation for the New World Order. But what is new about the New World Order? The institutionalized order is the same. The overall design is more technologically reinforced, more centralized and globalized, but basically the same. The institutional structures behind the politics are basically the same and the bureaucracies too, favoring institutions over individuals by just about how much locals will tolerate, basically the same now as it ever was wherever institutions took over the people. The institutional order of the world is the same as it ever was; oligarchical, pyramidal. The newness of the New World Order is not the order, it's the world, the polluted, increasingly toxic and radioactive netherworld.

The only newness about the world is our environment, our water, our air, the entirety of Earth Mother. It is newly depleted, polluted and has been everywhere marginalized and sporadically made permanently uninhabitable; Hanford, Chernobyl and Fukushima are a few of the more well-known locales permanently ruined and permanently releasing unfathomable poisons. The NWO is the abbreviation for the netherworld oligarchy, the result of billions of cannibalizing Wendigos.

The Wendigos have five claws of destruction. The longest claw, the worst source of environmental destruction in the netherworld oligarchy, perhaps the one most demanding of our immediate attention, is the claw of global nuclear experimentation. This includes the recent utilization of euphemistically named "depleted" uranium as ammunition, the hundreds of power generation experiments across the planet as well as the thousands of detonations which rained radioactive particles that ride the wind, saturate the atmosphere, freckle the soil and spark your very bones.

The second Wendigo claw of environmental destruction is global mining and burning fossil fuels; oil, natural gas and coal included. The nuclear era began the day the first nuke went off in New Mexico. The petrolithic era began the day Rudolph Diesel died. Rudolph Diesel designed his engine to be fueled with locally sourced biofuels or earthly sourced petroleum if locally available, so as to power localization, not to build up globalization. Diesel and his ideas mysteriously died at sea just prior to World War One.

The third Wendigo claw is the tendency to resource all our goods from digging up and cannibalizing Earth Mother. Mining leaves permanent ruin and spreads toxins far and wide. The plasticization of packaging and products has resulted in the throwaway society that poisons land and sea. Plastics are dug up petroleum products, replaceable with agricultural alternatives, particularly the conveniently illegal crop of hemp. Plastics are just another petroleum product of the petrolithic era, but plastic by itself, littered about like mined carbon, is as destructive to life as it is offensive. The plasticization of all our waters permanently poisons all, just as mining for minerals does.

The fourth Wendigo claw is the planetary war state. Nuclear experimentation as a whole could simply fall into this category, if it were not so insidiously destructive on its own when utilized for "civil" purposes. The conundrum of nuclear experimentation, spawned from war, reflects the same haunting problems of the planetary war state. The war state and nuclear experimentation both steal and kill. Both make all in the present poorer, destroy the environment and leave future death and horror. Both poison the present and the future. Both directly kill and indirectly degrade all. The war claw however enrolls a percentage of every generation and trains them into base thinking, basic training, in order to be forceful and obedient institutional tools.

The fifth claw of the Wendigo world, the opposable thumb if you will, is corporculture. The removal of the agriculture, permaculture and indigenous culture and the subsequent replacement with corporate factory farming is the worst aspect of this claw, infiltrating and degrading our very biology. However this claw represents the overall subjugation to institutions people vastly abide by. The very essence of our growing children and our sustenance has been transformed into a pay by the pound business, where nutrition is meaningless. Monsanto and DuPont among others have genetically modified our food, Earth Mother's intricate essence, mostly to withstand toxic pesticides which kill pests, and any creatures that go near the stuff, toxic pesticides they sell, that end up in us. Corporations also raise animals in overcrowded conditions resulting in hazards for the animals, the surrounding environment and belittled quality food around the world.

The five claws of the Wendigo world are controlled by an ill informed and ill minded collective. Each problem is rooted in selfish and misdirected thinking. Each of the claws on its own is horrendous and each related to the others. And each is rooted in our collective mind state. The destructive claws are the result of our real problem; ourselves.

The extraction and distribution of petrolithic and nuclear fuels are the primary polluters of Earth Mother, the primary destroyers of regions and likely the central initiation of the expanding cancer era. Plastics are petroleum product combined with chemicals. All energy and all plastic could be sourced from agriculture, in cooperation with Earth Mother instead of working against her. All our agricultural processes could be fashioned in a way that is cooperative with all Earth Mother's creatures, the creatures labeled as pests that ultimately the very soil is dependent on and integrated with, permaculture. However such systems would not be oligarchical, would not profit the few. There are always natural, viable choices beneficial to life however these are labeled as alternative because they would benefit everything instead of an elite few.

Perhaps war is ultimately the worst destroyer of Earth Mother and society. It's the greatest expander of environmental entropy and societal stagnancy no matter the weaponry. War causes destruction and leaves people unmotivated or incapable of helping Earth Mother or each other. Whether it is a war on terror or a war on drugs, or war wherever, all war is detrimental to the whole planet and all war limits the quality life of everyone, harming and hindering even future generations.

The fast food lifestyle, the live-to-eat mentality is destroying the planet and increasing the culture of separation. We eat food of unknown origin from plastic containers without knowing where they'll end up. Such consumption without consideration is destroying the world. It's parasitic. Conventional monoculture and genetic modification based on allowing mega doses of petrochemical sourced pesticides is likely killing you and probably causing biological impact on the ecosystem comparable to horror movies. Genetic modification is as dangerous as nuclear experimentation altering our very DNA.

Each of the five claws of the Wendigo are interrelated like sinews of a claw. The most stark and main commonality; they are oligarchical to the Nth degree, to the Netherworld degree. All these systems benefit a few and cost entirely. These operations are so deadly they cost all future generations yet unborn, pockmarking the world with cancer clusters. All life will pay environmental costs basically forever, this is the NWO; the netherworld oligarchy.

"A rocky vineyard does not need a prayer, but a pick ax." ~Navajo saying

The environmental destruction, generations in the making, caused by burning fossil fuels, nuclear fuels, warring, mining and corporculture, will cost future generations in the most oligarchical form imaginable; biologically. Long dead oligarchs were made wealthy while generations will suffer dirtied waters, toxic land and loaded air. An oligarchy was made and cost generations of strangers through the destroyed environment. The world order is the same pyramidal construct only in a devastated environment, a netherworld oligarchy to the Nth degree, the NWO.

The culture of separation built the netherworld oligarchy. A mind in fear will separate itself from everything. And when separated in fear the claws of the Wendigo can easily latch onto you spiritually or literally speaking. The near hollow and shallow collective mentality essentially living by the mantra 'it is not my problem' allowed institutions to take control, because of fear. We separated ourselves from Earth Mother, from each other, from our own and from other rich cultures, we separated ourselves from agriculture and fresh water. We separated ourselves from our seed, we allow chemical corporations to genetically modify food to be poisonous to 'pests' instead of integrating our systems to benefit entirety, instead of demanding healthy nutritious food. We live in a fearful culture of separation, providing unlimited flesh for the Wendigos.

The culture of separation began long before 9/11, but 9/11 cemented it. There are many layers to this calamity, but the main psychological catapult was when the President of the U.S.A. suggested people literally go shopping after the event, to not change. The worst crime in history, the worst terrorist attack ever had just taken place in Manhattan in unison with an attack on the Pentagon and we should simply stabilize the economy. Should we question and investigate or change our course? Nope. Just go shopping. And with that the culture of separation was cemented.

The Occupy Wall Street movement is the first political groundswell of the 21st century to captivate and catalyze people across the world and one of the first to quantify and confront the ubiquitous culture of separation and the Wendigos. Despite the complexity of the institutionalization Occupy Wall Street is 100% correct. 1% are reaping from and keeping down the 99% through immoral means in the netherworld oligarchy. 1% over 99% is the exact formation of traditional pyramidal oligarchies. And whatever part of the world you may go, the ratio is about that, 1% over 99% -overtly.

The netherworld oligarchy, the cronyism of global corporatism is exponentially oligarchical through the total environmental destruction. Every human is subjected to further expense, hardship and taxation because of the environmental calamity. Whole generations are being born into a toxic environment perpetuated by oligarchs. All future life all around the world will have some radioactive particulate originating in Chernobyl and Fukushima as part of our biology. The unborn of the unborn will pay the former USSR and TEPCO -forever.

All institutions digging up the guts of Earth Mother are oligarchical in the most extreme manner and subdue her into the netherworld. The demonstrative 1% profit from the extraction, refinement and distribution of these resources and the 99% pay them for it. Before the material is used it damages the area from where it came, the fuels are then burned resulting in further environmental damage and accidents occur all blatantly poisoning us now and future generations. And people don't see it because of the culture of separation and the fear to look at ourselves. The netherworld oligarchy institutions tax us a hundred generation fold, to the point that Occupy Wall Street is correct in theory, only off by an order of magnitude a thousand or so, to the point maybe something like 0.0000000001% truly benefit from the global environmental destruction we will face. In the netherworld oligarchy everyone will pay with their health for a dead stranger's wealth.

"The frog does not drink up the pond in which he lives." ~ Sioux proverb

The global environmental destruction for profit benefitted the few and costs everyone, now and forever. The level of future environmental taxation is up to us to slow and cease. The netherworld oligarchy is an environmentally devastated Earth Mother controlled by the same institutionally dominant formations which have always been, only now technologically reinforced and globalized, only now in a disfigured environment, a netherworld.

The netherworld oligarchy controls most effectively when it is not perceived, when it's unconsidered. The main difference between people today and people one thousand years ago is that people today are more likely to roll over and submit to polluted water, air, land and sea. People today are more likely to allow total corruption, to the point that Earth Mother is forever negatively altered, if not a dying Gaia, to the point we'll accept injecting poison rather than stand up for our very biological self. Today people assume they are being poisoned and that everything's corrupt and do nothing.

We allow toxic experimental fertilizers and pesticides to be applied to our growing food and called conventional. We allow chemical concoctions in our food, substances which are indeed not food and not good for self to be included in our diet. Many chemicals used in U.S.A. food have been banned elsewhere. Many nations have banned genetically modified organisms to feed to their animals and people, whereas most in the center of the culture of separation care not or about what they consume. The U.S.A. allowed chemical companies, Monsanto in particular, to genetically modify plants so that they might gross more money. Most sugar is derived from genetically modified beets, a substance that looks like beet, tastes like beet, but is not beet. A simple way to understand the difference between agriculture and genetic modification is agricultural breeds vertically with plant and like plant to produce offspring down the line. Genetic modification breeds horizontally with bits of plants, animals and bacteria strewn together in hopes it will line up okay.

We yield control to the point we'll accept genetic modification of our food, pesticides, hormones, confined livestock and an artificial sweetener instead of honey or maple. The Native American Indians revered corn. The Wendigos stole Turtle Island and their corn and ultimately, practically, ruined it all, the land, the water, the air and even the intricate essence of the revered corn seed. To the American Indians corn was synonymous with man and it has been genetically altered, genetically stolen and removed.

Human society is more complacent to mind manipulation and environmental destruction now than at any time before. And in contrast the oligarchies are more complicit in corruption and destruction than at any time before. We are so subdued we accept food that is not food prepared so as to better pay a franchise corporation, and we will shrug our shoulders as if there is nothing to do about it when generations are being literally and effectively fed poison and imprisoned and bombs are dropping.

Part of our fear, essential to keeping the culture of separation is keeping the human race doomstruck. The end of the Mayan Calendar is one of many circulated stories to keep the collective mind state on the impending apocalypse, to keep us doomstruck. The doomstruck mind state likely has deep psychological roots, but is promoted by the symposium of death cults and religions that have been trumpeting the looming doom for eons, not the Mayan Calendar. Why? Why is the fascination with death and total end promoted? We might be simply fascinated with death. But humans are malleable. We can be shaped to hold many perspectives and interests, not just of death and not just in one way. We are influenced to think about certain things in certain ways. The perspective that the end is coming in 1999, 2000, 2012, 2013, etcetera keeps everyone from considering what's really going on, our own suicidal self-destructive behavior. Only now since the beginning of postmodernism, because of the NWO, is such an apocalyptic ending scenario possible.

The real reason for the fascination with apocalyptic death might very well be so as to distract us from our destructive ways, our negative shadow. The fascination with death is a distraction from doing anything about the very real precipice we have built our society on, one where every earthquake, every hurricane and every lightning storm might result in permanent regional destruction. Ours is a world where writing a bucket list of things to do before you die is acceptable rather than being inspired to make positive change before you die. The majority of humanity would rather watch the big game or go bungee jumping rather than consider the state of the world and take action in it. The precarious design of our world is totally deadly and yet we are too complacent to do anything about it, even consider it. We have become the shrug your shoulders society, burdened with the belief that we are all doomed anyway and there is nothing we can do about it so why bother to do anything, but cheat time for a momentary glimpse at happiness, a taste of aged wine and tender beef.

"Do not speak of evil for it creates curiosity in the hearts of the young." ~Lakota Proverb

This doomstruck attitude of futility is pervasive the world over. And it's no accident. People would rather sit through destruction of totality in order to check off something from their bucket list than stand up, whereas just a hundred years ago people would duel with pistols over the disrespect of a lady. Today individuals tolerate the five Wendigo claws of faceless institutions. Our world has been turned upside down from a place of beauty and availability to a place where the only untainted resources are controlled by the netherworld oligarchies which created the environmental problem to begin with. And most individuals uphold or yield to their authority.

The only way to stand up to the Netherworld oligarchies and heal Earth Mother is to stand together, like arrows bound in peace, but the world is doomstruck, so obsessed with selfish bucket lists and distorted personal fetishes we're apathetic to the fact that everyone is bound in a shared predicament. We are all in this together. When we stand together as spiritual brothers, alive and here at the same time, we can begin to heal Earth Mother. Obviously having a duel is excessive and ridiculous, but standing up for Earth Mother is a righteous undertaking. Standing up for a tree or anything your heart holds dear is righteous based on heartfelt decision. Your heart will never steer you wrong if your mind doesn't get in the way and if the ideas of others don't subvert you. All brave souls who fastened themselves to trees and the machines to tear them down did so because they felt love. Loving kindness and caring for Earth Mother is greater than any other ideal. Standing together for real heartfelt care like saving a tree instead of airy laws promoting the netherworld oligarchy is more valid than supporting any institutional jargon backed by any law.

"Hold on to what is good, even if it's a handful of earth. Hold on to what you believe, even if it's a tree that stands by itself. Hold on to what you must do, even if it's a long way from here. Hold on to your life, even if it's easier to let go. Hold on to my hand, even if someday I'll be gone away from you." ~Pueblo Prayer

Our doomstruck apathy, our minds leading our hearts, allows the netherworld oligarchy. Our greatest power as individuals among institutions is our perspective and our ability to work together. In fact humanity would still be field snacks if it wasn't for our ability to work together and form unique perspectives through asking new questions. But today many are so tolerant of institutional wrongdoing we'll forego our power and accept being fed genetically modified poisoned apples from serpents without question. The collective of humanity have also abandoned the brotherhood of man. We have forgotten about the power we have individually and when we stand together. There is no animal on the field and no institution in the world which can hold back people who work together.

Sometimes all people need is a symbol to shift their perception, like a tree or rock or anything used in the right manner at the right time. Protests and political movements, activists and inactivists create and destroy symbols. The Y 12 Three could have painted the uranium storage building with spray paint, instead they chose baby bottles filled with blood. The Boston Tea Party was a symbolic destruction of real property, real tea in a similar symbolic manner. The tea toss served to inspire, or contribute to the inspiration to abandon the British East India Company and the worldwide parliamentary monarchy of the UK. The destruction of the Berlin Wall was symbolic for and arguably led to collapse of the Soviet Union. The United Soviet Socialist Republic, a vast nuclear nation, crumbled after the Berlin Wall was taken down with sledgehammers. First came the Chernobyl disaster in April, 1986, the Berlin Wall fell in 1989 and the U.S.S.R. dissolved in 1991.

"One finger cannot lift a pebble." ~Hopi saying

"He who would do great things should not attempt them all alone." ~Seneca proverb

Individuals united can remove and remake global empires on which the sun never sets and nuclear nations armed with the power of the sun, simply through joining together and realizing their potential power in peace. No institution can stop informed and motivated individuals.

Behind the scenes of revolution, whether governmental or technological, there are often discreet powers playing roles as instigators or detractors so as to benefit in one way or another. Revolution serves individuals and is therefore must be peaceful, war serves institutions and costs individuals. A little green revolution would simply require individuals come together in clarity and brotherhood. The only way to heal Earth Mother is to stop fighting each other and stop fighting to be on top of the pyramid system. Revolution of the mind state is required and can be instigated with the proper creation or destruction of symbols.

The creation and destruction of symbols is crucial to inspire enough peaceful revolutionary individuals (normally just 5% is needed) and counter the destruction of Earth Mother. And even though there are often other extraordinary powers which play important roles in revolution it is up to the people how it proceeds. The U.S.S.R. might still exist if it weren't for the economic crash at least partially employed by foreign intelligence agencies if not outright instigated, but it is ultimately up to individuals. Oil went from over sixty dollars a barrel to about twenty during this time. The crashing Soviet economy was encouraged to do so by those that could benefit. No matter the outside influences that contributed to the downfall of the U.S.S.R. the Wendigos which are killing us all really killed the U.S.S.R.; nuclear experimentation, dependence on oil and war. Each is ill for national and individual livelihood.

Institutions are built to provide for people and structure under which be protected. Institutions pretend to be harvestable trees, that with water and care, or resources and workers, one might be able to harvest from, but frequently institutional fruit is a figurative carrot on a stick leading us astray. Most institutions are dependent on national institutions because nations control property, like vines or undergrowth. The national institution trees extoll their virtues for the many, but predominantly benefit the few. National institutions grow and induce a lush garden to grow around it. But when exposed to the desertification of nuclear experimentation, petroleum dependence and war most all trees die, real and institutional. Institutional trees require vast amounts of resources and people, but always are promoted as benefitting many. The bigger the tree the more it becomes concerned with its roots and branches rather than the leaves or birds or other ants and plants here and there. The bigger the tree the more there are who might be aware of its fruit and the more outside influences might consider taking it down aside from those revolutionaries who simply want to build or destroy some symbol so as to raise awareness and elevate comprehension.

"18 Early in the morning, as Jesus was on his way back to the city, he was hungry. 19 Seeing a fig tree by the road, he went up to it but found nothing on it except leaves. Then he said to it, "May you never bear fruit again!" Immediately the tree withered. 20 When the disciples saw this, they were amazed. "How did the fig tree wither so quickly?" they asked. 21 Jesus replied, "Truly I tell you, if you have faith and do not doubt, not only can you do what was done to the fig tree, but also you can say to this mountain, 'Go, throw yourself into the sea,' and it will be done. 22 If you believe, you will receive whatever you ask for in prayer."

~Mathew 21:18-22

Institutional trees, whether a global monarchy run by King George and the B.E.I.C. or a nuclear super power like U.S.S.R., are all in fact entirely dependent on individuals and can be changed at any time. Institutions are not individuals and may, as machines, exist infinitely longer than individuals, thousands of years. But institutional trees no matter how petrified in society, no matter if they have the root structure of aspens or the enormity of redwoods, can be removed, situations replanted, fruit redistributed at any time for individuals are in control. Real trees can be planted where there was once marble and only proverbial benefit and hyperbole progress.

The Little Green Book of Revolution is a gardener's manual for modern times. It is an explanation of the powers at the disposal of the doomstruck in a culture of separation, written in celebration of the American Indian renaissance to inspire sustainable living. It is for the artists and activists, the creators and destroyers of symbols, the rainbow warriors for Earth Mother. The Little Green Book of Revolution is a presentation of revolutionary understanding for the 99% born into the netherworld oligarchy.

The Little Green Book is written to inspire individual activism or inactivism, the artists, the 5%, the positive and proactive of the 99% who understand and initiate. The 5% principal is a powerful political idea as well as conservationist and fund raising idea. If people stop just 5% of their wrongdoing, i.e. pollution and exploitive consumption favoring institutions of the netherworld oligarchy, we could make a difference in whatever direction is focused. If people donated just 5% of their income and 5% of their time or focused idea the combination of 5% soon magnifies into figures institutions cannot deny.

5% is considered to be a tipping point. New trends, be they fashion or technology or any other idea, usually take a while to accept. Even with quality marketing, and advertising investment, it may take a long time for one percent to turn into two percent and two percent to turn into four percent, but when five percent is reached growth accelerates exponentially.

The 5% have changed the world. Those who sought colonial independence in 1773 were said to be about 5% or less of the population. The vast majority thought whoever would challenge the Crown were bloody batty. The original patriots, those who threw the Boston Tea Party, were at first a minority among the majority who believed their actions were mad or futile.

The ideas of the 5% are often so counter to the status quo, so revolutionary, that initially their numbers remain below 5%. Civil rights in the U.S.A. were enabled by the 5%. Nelson Mandela changed the world, at first with a minority of 5%. Perestroika and Glasnost, the Velvet Revolution, the liberty experienced in Eastern Europe, the fall of the Berlin Wall and the U.S.S.R. were all initiated by the catalystic 5%.

The 5% have always initiated revolutions of the mind state so as to spur revolution of how we operate. Malcolm X was a civil rights activist who was assassinated. He believed that individuals ought to protect and defend themselves, he did not believe violence was a solution. He did believe that if individuals were being unreasonably attacked by anybody including uniformed police officers that they ought to fight back as a living and breathing being.

Perhaps the only people who should not fight back if attacked are the builders and destroyers of symbols so as to ensure the symbol is built or destroyed in the most righteous manner. Gandhi freed all of South Asia in a peaceful movement which took all the abuse that was offered and made the authorities look like the evil enslavers they were. Builders and destroyers often must ascend violence and thievery or anything else which might undermine the symbolism, just as no one was allowed to steal the tea at the Boston Tea Party.

One of Malcolm X's students started The Nation of Gods and Earths in Harlem soon after Malcolm was assassination. It is a movement, based on teaching youth in the streets. It is often confused with a religion, but it is not a religion. One of the most prominent and well known lessons of The Nation of Gods an Earths breaks down the percentages that equate the longtime status quo of the pyramidal oligarchy and our dumbed down culture of separation.

The theory is that 85% of people are lost, misled and manipulated, ignorantly killing themselves without knowing who they really are. And the 10% are the exploiters and enslavers of the poor and lost. The 10% are responsible for and benefit from the manipulation of the 85%. Lastly there is the 5%, who attempt to do the right thing and free the minds of the 85%. The 85% are known as the dumb, deaf and blind. The 10% are referred to as the slave makers of the poor. And the 5% are the poor righteous teachers.

"Five percent of the people think; ten percent of the people think they think; and the other eighty five percent would rather die than think."
~Thomas Edison

The 10% manipulate and benefit off of the 85%. And the 5% attempt free the minds of the 85% from the 10%. Within the 10% is another societal Mandelbrot fractal of the same dimension as the original ratio. There is a 10% of the 10%, equating to the 1% of the total. A 1% exactly as equated by the Occupy Wall Street movement. The 1% are the main instigators and perpetrators of deception to rule over the 85%, and the 99%.

Peaceful revolution is possible and accomplished when the 10% allow the 85% to follow the 5% out of their proverbial cave without repercussions. Peaceful change is possible when people are unafraid to stop and go as they wish and not as they are made to, when institutions let go. Peaceful revolution is possible when the 10% cannot convince the 85% to react violently in attempts to keep the status quo and eliminate the 5%.

It is impossible to extract oneself physically from the environment of the netherworld oligarchy and seemingly impossible to extract oneself from the status quo supportive of the 10%. But it is possible. All the 85% and some of the 10% do not know they are killing themselves, ourselves. We are all easily steered in the wrong direction, but realization if this can be enough measure of prevention. Sometimes the equations of actuality are easily put together. But that is only if we consider actuality in the first place.

10% over the 85% and 5% is certainly an oligarchy, expounded to the next level, the 10% become the 1%, which is oligarchical to about the normal order of magnitude. Multiply that by the environmental costs individuals face because some oligarchical businessman in the distant past used arsenic on his cotton fields or dispersed poisons in mining for gold reducing a once lush area's waterways for generations, creating the netherworld oligarchy and you get the netherworld oligarchy of the some odd 00000000.1%.

When the 85% and the 99% learn they are killing themselves, they will start to question and take action. Only when the majority understands the netherworld oligarchy will the status quo can be changed. As long as we continue to go about in culture of separation, fulfilling bucket lists ignoring the heartfelt there will be no change. And because of the extensive capability the oligarchies have in regard to mediation of the masses, because the controlling authorities prevent consideration of actuality, revolutionaries construct and destroy symbols to rattle the attention of the masses, of the some odd 99.000000099%.

"I do not think the measure of a civilization is, how tall its buildings of concrete are, but rather how well its people have learned to relate to their environment and fellow man." ~Sun Bear of the Chippewa Tribe

Individuals and Institutions

The collective mind of mankind is malleable. We can be trained to think we are nothing but response mechanisms like Gila Monsters with only a few predictable reactions to various different pokes and prods. We can be trained to exist in institutional trees akin to prisons. We can be tricked to exist in total slavery and tricked into dismantling our own hopes and dreams so they are nothing but forgotten nocturnal whispers. We can be trained and tricked into giving up all that is human and humane, into killing others and sacrificing ourselves on behalf of an institutional tree bearing no fruit. We can be trained to think that the world, as it is now, is normal. Or we can train ourselves to find our true nature. We are trained directly and indirectly, in ways we notice and in ways we do not, less so when we train ourselves.

Jesus Christ was a peaceful revolutionary. Whether you want to call his story a nice allegory or holy word of god doesn't matter to how influential his story is. Jesus was one of the best builders and destroyer of symbols ever and was so committed to revolution, he sacrificed himself as a symbol to be destroyed, arguably on lone level to inspire people and notify them of the wrongdoing of the institutions in The Temple. Jesus was crucified because he rattled the institutional order, he shook the tree, much in the same way as Socrates allowed himself to be sentenced to death, to bring attention to the institutionalization.

Recently Wilhelm Reich allowed himself to be tried, convicted and imprisoned, eventually dying in jail, to be destroyed as a symbol. He invented healing machines and promoted the idea of sexual healing among other, now heavily redacted and contraband ideas. Wilhelm Reich believed that maintenance of our sexual energy, orgone, was the key to health and longevity. He wasn't alone of course as ancient Taoist texts and yogi philosophy speak of developing and harnessing sexual energy and turning it into life energy –only through meditative movement rather than machinery.

Wilhelm Reich authored several books and invented several machines which were acclaimed for their healing powers and distained for discussing healing sexual energy among puritan sentimentality, in a culture of separation so insistent the discussion of sex was limited. Eventually, despite the First Amendment, his writing and healing inventions were banned and he suffered seeing his books turned to ashes in the biggest book burning in U.S.A. history. The U.S.A Government, through the FDA, sued and jailed him, because he crossed a line with his orgone accumulator. He died in 1957 sure that he would be vindicated and his imprisonment, himself a destroyed symbol, would spur a cultural revolution against restricting actuation of healing and sexual feeling. Today you can purchase orgonite variously and find the schematics to various healing inventions of his. Orgonite theory basically involves combing metals with organic materials to initiate gathering of positive energy and elimination of negative energy. Because Wilhelm went against the oligarchical grain of institutions and because he spoke of sexual taboo, he was restricted from practice, sued for continuing to practice and jailed.

The Vietnamese Buddhist monk Thich Quang Duc self-immolated himself and burned to death in the lotus meditation position. Thich Quang Duc burned himself in 1963 as a symbol to call attention to what he saw as religious inequality and institutional exploitation conducted by the controlling government.

Under great distress from the weight of similar feelings of institutional repression Mohamed Bouazizi set himself afire in December 2010 in order to call attention to his predicament. The Tunisian fruit vendor became the symbol and destroyed himself, instigating the Tunisian Revolution and setting the stage for the Arab Spring. He did so because the institution confiscated his goods because he could not pay tariffs. Mohamed set himself afire in front of a government office sparking protests and government change across borders.

In November, 2012 several Tibetan Buddhist monks, just teenagers, set themselves on fire in front of a police station to protest Chinese rule. The Tibetan monks want a free Tibet and the return of their exiled spiritual leader the Dalai Lama. They face the same repressive rule of institutions restricting religious celebration and life. The immolations in Tibet spurred more government restriction.

The most powerful revolutionary actions or inactions cause the harshest institutional reactions which in turn raise awareness to the problem. Harsh reactions against revolution are meant to quell movements, but might swell them. Knocking over the right table in the temple like Jesus, teaching the youths on the street like Socrates or inventing new healing machines and procedures are the best things you can do for humanity and prevent the eventual burst of emotional duress that would make one choose self-immolation as opposed to finding the right thing to toss over at the right time.

Whatever the specific nuances, whatever the location where millions are gathering in the street, revolution today is individuals versus institutions netherworld oligarchy, the worldwide war economy and police state, the same corruption and restriction that is in Tunisia or China and the U.S.A.; usually about as much as the particular collective will tolerate. There is no time in the revolution of the war economy, which represses all of humanity, that violence should be considered. Violence infiltrates any activity, but everyone must do their best to come together to realize it is institutions versus individuals, institutionalized versus indigenous. For revolution no one should hurt others or themselves. There are always better symbols to destroy than oneself or others. Inspire resolution and revolution without bloodshed by thinking about tossing the right tables at the right time and teaching the right person the right thing. Institutions can poison and jail and quiet anyone, but they really only slow the inevitable evolution or revolution when one is open and peaceful. One need not be as drastic as Thich or Mohamed, in fact if one is half as committed as these revolutionaries you mustn't hurt yourself. There are far too few of you.

Instead yell! Instead tackle their tables, rattle their trees and teach the youth what heart is, instead destroy a symbol besides one that is living, instead build one.

There is a distinct difference between institutional propaganda, for war or otherwise, and the individual use of symbols, for peace or otherwise. It is as distinct as the difference between a real fig tree and an office branch, between a living breathing being and an institution. Institutions use propaganda to steer many and to produce fruit, normally for an elite few. And institutions always hide the fact they are producing propaganda, acting like it is reality unaltered. Individuals who construct and destroy symbols do so to bring light to the actions of others and promote the fact they are doing so to obtain the attention of people who are being lied to and exploited.

Institutions do whatever they can to hide the fact they steer thinking so as to fasten their controlling grip. Activists do whatever they can to reveal the fact they act to expose the controlling institutions to loosen their hold. The stronghold on the presentation of information is the same now as it ever was, only there is much more information. The controlling institutions accumulate information so as to maintain their encasement, to better present their case. And yet one could present facts to support anything. It's all a matter of sources and which factors are considered. And so revolutionaries first decide with heartfelt compassion and then seek out the facts for the heart's reasoning. Institutions influence our thinking with their facts and ignore our hearts. Be a revolutionary, do not let facts steer your heart for facts are frequently lies by omission; 100% true, just not 100% of the truth. Do not let institutional facts steer your heart. The Hopi speak of the Two-hearts, having taken on the hunger of another. Do not adopt the heart of an institution.

Controlling institutions nearly always end up being repressive, normally out of fear that the tree they grew will no longer be needed and so they lie to maintain it, with facts. It's basic human nature only expressed by machines. People seek to gain, however a more powerful motivator can be to not incur losses on one's gains. Today the oligarchy is the same, only with more to lose and more technology to use with Earth Mother abused.

Revolutionaries, builders and destroyers of symbols, seek changes and in change, there are losses. The status quo shifts and today the wagon wheel business is not what it used to be. The losers in technological and societal revolutions usually have it coming somehow. The losers no longer provide a useful role, or perhaps never did. A revolution is not war, a revolution is a rotation, or counter rotation, a turning of the tides. Today we need revolution to change the polluting warring culture of separation resulting in hindrance to our physical and mental wellbeing. Once it was the wagon wheel, tomorrow we could stop building nuclear experiments or war machines or prisons.

Revolution is change. War is war, two different words with two different meanings. War maintains the status quo, whereas revolution turns it. The status quo is cemented by seriously rigid institutions that do not want change. But the wagon wheel industry could not stop automobiles. Eventually the oligarchical institutions of today, no matter how they war to maintain the status quo, no matter how they try to steer our thinking, will also fall be the wayside, either with us all as sinking ship, or on their own, a skeleton to rebuild a reef system.

The environmental tipping point is upon us. The world requires the collective turns back before the environmental tipping point occurs, so as to save ourselves from ourselves, from global nuclear experimentation, petrolithic fire and the counterproductive oligarchical mining of Earth Mother. If agricultural sourced energy, like hemp oil or endless energy systems, like sun, wind, wave and ocean current technology are not implemented the netherworld oligarchy will be cemented for future generations. 400 parts of carbon dioxide per million in the air will steadily increase and birthrates will decrease. The reason we all do not have more resources is because of old oligarchical tendencies to grow institutional trees to benefit the few over the many instead of gardens for all. The first requirement for change is information distribution, take the information that you have and distribute it into the garbage. We must turn inward to the heart. Information is easily distorted and can be used to lead us astray. Society is so influenced we are sometimes trained with information. Your potential friends are labeled enemies. Alternatives are labeled alternative because they are not oligarchical enough, not because they don't work. Systems presented as unacceptable are often the best way, but are interpreted as being counterproductive because they counterexploitive and society is like a very sure adolescent with limited information. But even children in their hearts cannot be steered wrong with institutional information.

The reason our industry is environmentally destructive is because it's designed to operate in support of the netherworld oligarchy, a pyramidal system of the few over the many. The institutional trees were set up that way because they are efficient at producing wealth. We are trained to be motivated to capitalize on everybody in oligarchical fashion and to allow it. We have the technology to all be free, the problem is the oligarchy.

"It has become appallingly obvious that our technology has exceeded our humanity." ~Albert Einstein

There is an old netherworld joke; capitalism is man taking advantage of man and communism is the opposite of that. A return to indigenous ways is needed not yielding to institutional trees. Localization is needed not globalization, a return to the circle of life. We are taught our whole life to sit down, shut up and stay out of it. Institutions quell consideration of integration and revolution. Practically all institutional tradition celebrates prevention of revolution and the culture of separation. We are taught to sit in a row, stand in line and form orderly productive units that follow rules. We are subtly trained to think of ourselves as separate from everyone and everything.

Society is structured in a way that to even speak about revolution is taboo. Refusal to stop killing each other on behalf of millennia old institutions inspires accusations of ignorance. Revolution is not war, the world is at war and has been at war for a thousand years. A revolution would be peace. One of the main differences between indigenous culture and institutional civilization is the buildup of war culture to the point we can destroy entirety.

Revolution seeks peace and evolution, war is war. War stagnates, revolution turns. In a war economy where nations spend more on metal and explosives than they do on mothers, peace is revolution. The world is trained to war, to look at interactions as a war and to especially react as if at war when anybody presents something revolutionary.

Those who oppose institutional abuse of the status quo are resented – because people are trained to react that way. Those who question and protest police abuse of authority, the buildup of Orwellian surveillance and a constant state of war on terrorism and drugs, might be ostracized because people are trained. The conscientious objectors of WW1 could be compared with people shouting, 'fuck the police' because of police violence, drug prohibition and construction of jails rather than schools. Today the war claw of the Wendigo world attacks through narcotic prohibition, the war on terror and technological surveillance of all. Drug prohibition creates an outlet to construct an extensive prison system, just as war policy creates terrorism to war on. The world needs teachers not cops. We need information to move forward, we don't need to be watch and held back.

Institutional infrastructure is primarily, no matter how explained otherwise, installed to maintain itself and its position in the netherworld oligarchy, by force. Forceful authorities are built to prevent revolution, to prevent those afflicted in the netherworld from confronting an oligarch. Global drug prohibition enabled the beginning of constant war and the war on terrorism arguably amplified it and definitely amplified war.

Institutions use war for stability, but war is stagnancy or end for individuals. Institutions promote war as being for the greater good specifically and indirectly. Everybody learns how many great medical discoveries were made during war, for instance. It's not that war leads to technological or medical discovery it is that war is the technological focus which led to discovery. To see the positive in the killing fields is training.

Revolution is peace, the status quo is war. The destruction of the environment in war through institutions like the euphemistically named

Department of Defense is the status quo. Economic stability is put above environmental sustainability and political ideology is put above living beings. We are trained to be confrontational and ignorant to the fact that war on one is war on us all. We war on people foreign and domestic with violations of the most basic precepts of liberty suggested in the Magna Carta and cemented in the Bill of Rights. We war on or imagine warring on everyone, in business, in relationships and policy. We are trained to be apathetic to watching it and joining it.

Just preparing for war is an insanely deadly environmental abomination. Over two thousand known atomic and thermonuclear detonations have been sparked just to see what would happen. These detonations have scorched the Earth and atmosphere with radioactive particulate. The netherworld oligarchy reaps reward from war, nothing more benefits.

Institutional interests are controlling. Institutions at the behest of individuals clench onto the status quo and everyone in it becomes an experiment to those ends, nuclear experimentation, genetic modification of plants, trees, animals and viruses are some of the most Pandoric procedures to take greedy control. The impulse to question or react is there, but because people are trained, encased in the culture of separation. Most are so afraid of revolution they will allow chemical corporations to transform the seed of their into franchise product. No creature would transform food into something dependent on large quantities of toxic chemicals -unless sick. Only Two-hearts would build up a franchise tree to sell toxins, design a tree bearing no fruit. Only a chemical corporation would transform wholesome food into something else and only the culture of separation would allow it. Agriculture, the heart of human culture, is increasingly corporate monoculture.

No healthy being would build nuclear weapons and practice open genetic modification based on toxins. Only individuals in complete fear and isolation would yield sovereignty to nuclear experimentation and genetic modification. Only beings held in fear would ever maintain complacency to the Wendigo claws. We, as a global collective, exist in fear of standing up for what is right, fear of revolution. The reason Jesus is worshipped the world over and the reason Socrates is unparalleled as a philosopher is because they were revolutionaries without fear. Jesus revolted against the oligarchical links of church and state, Socrates revolted against the oligarchical education system with the state.

The Two-hearts and the fake trees posing as real trees, the masquerading institutional mirages have been at war with individuals since their beginning. It's always been individuals versus institutions. For Jesus it was traditionalists versus the compassionate, for Socrates it was elitist sophistry versus open information for all, but the individual rising up against the institution is central to many prophets and philosophers both. Jesus cursed the old world oligarchical collectivists in the temple. Socrates told them all to be damned too. It's individuals versus institutions and always has been. Institutions retain the culture of separation to keep individuals stagnant, revolution is individual evolution.

Nietzsche posed that the only way people might cross the barren chasm between the sheepish masses and elevated consciousness, to become uberman was to step up and face those who were cursing and affronting Earth Mother and others living here. To transform oneself from just one of the masses controlled by herders, first one has to stand up and face the doomstruck and the herders. The following quotes are from Thus Spoke Zarathustra.

"One repays a teacher badly if one always remains nothing but a pupil."

"But it is the same with man as with the tree. The more he seeks to rise into the height and light, the more vigorously do his roots struggle earthward, downward, into the dark, the deep - into evil."

"You say that a good cause will even sanctify war! I tell you, it is the good war that sanctifies every cause!"

At the essence of human dynamics is a tendency toward institutionalization or individuation, toward building up oligarchy or liberty. Through the lens of Thus Spoke Zarathustra, Nietzsche posited man was on a rope over a chasm, on one side the animalistic and on the other the conscious uberman, on one side the sheep and the coyotes and on the other side the noble attuned individual, like the archetypal American Indian. We are stuck on a rope, capable of going forward or backward or just sitting there, capable of barbaric behavior or of a highly developed and attuned being. It is your duty to cross the chasm, your duty to answer the call to consciousness.

"Today the species of Man is facing a question of the very survival of the species. The way of life known as Western Civilization is on a death path… Our essential message to the world is a basic call to consciousness… The technologies and social systems which have destroyed the animal and plant life are also destroying the native people." ~Haudenosaunee, Call to Consciousness, 1977

Socrates' broke down the political and individual predicament in The Allegory of the Cave. It symbolizes that same search for consciousness from dullness. In the Allegory of the Cave there are prisoners, captors and the freed prisoner who tries to inform the others after being released and acquiring understanding that they are all stuck in a cave. They do not even know their predicament and watch and talk about only shadows. The Allegory of the Cave explores how we perceive and how we can be misled and closed off.

Hegel boiled down the human dynamic and found the master and slave similar to Nietzsche's uberman, both resonating the model of the Allegory of the Cave. The Master Slave Dialectic explores what happens politically and individually. It's a historical tale of society and allegory of individual consciousness weaved into one in a dualistic thesis. Hegel presented the history of revolution as a history of the state and the state of consciousness equating individual and collective development.

Hegel's Master Slave Dialectic explores inner and outer revolution. There are two different people representing two different cultures and two sides to an individual, representing individual and collective consciousness. Hegel observed history and noted when two different cultures meet one is superior to the other and either overtly or for all extents and purposes enslaves the other. Historically this is evident for this is the dynamic oligarchy functions on, in opposition. We all can relate to having two opposing sides within, the ego that wants and the consciousness that wills the animalistic impulsive and the higher conscious contemplative.

Revolution takes place in the streets of the nation state, but first in the hallways of the mind state. Hegel's story of revolution starts with the story of revolt against the Egyptian pharaohs and continues on through to the French revolution. All revolution begins as revolution inside the min, individual consciousness develops and then mass consciousness develops with it or there is confrontation, Hegel noted. A revolutionary development of consciousness today would be to simply be aware of the Master Slave dynamic, then abandon it.

The Master Slave Dialectic is a window into the psychological repression, the inner walls we build to maintain the inner status quo. We all have our own master which keeps us from freeing ourselves of old habits and old thinking. Only when our inner master is confronted by our inner slave is development possible. We all are subject to this psychological interplay inside and we are subject to the same in the outside world. Only when the actual slave stands up to the master is their development, revolution contains evolution.

The master keeps the slave in check and as long as the slave continues to be a slave the dynamic is static. Only when the slave revolts and refuses to obey, is the master forced to recognize the slave as an individual and then a possible confrontation erupts. Only when the slave revolts does he recognize his autonomy.

The master either takes on a violent struggle or releases the slave. This is why revolution is most often associated with war. There can be peaceful resolution, a revolution with or without struggle. Peaceful revolution occurs when both parties accept each other as equal autonomous individuals. Hegel posits many possibilities; the master might recognize the slave and there could be a peaceful end or there might be struggle, but in the end whoever wins the struggle each recognizes the other.

Revolution occurs inside the mind then outside. If the inside or outside state does not relinquish to the revolution of consciousness a confrontation ensues. Hegel pointed out the revolutions of the world all progressed individual and mass consciousness. Since the end of the French Revolution the dialectical slave has revolted a thousand times and the master has battled almost every time. The revolution is always of the mind and then the nation.

My father didn't punish me exceptionally harshly at all, but he did lock me in my room for something like half an hour, to cool off. Only when I figured out how to unlock the door with a butter knife did he stop punishing me. It was a nonviolent revolution of master and slave, my dad respected me as an autonomous individual who could now undo the lock. Authorities act to prevent revolution. Parents do so legitimately and with the right intentions. Institutions do so as if legitimate often with the sole intention of retaining control over individuals.

"There can never be peace between nations until there is first known that true peace which is within the souls of men." ~Black Elk

Institutional collectives can be understood as individual personas. Some institutions, like individuals, are more developed than others, some are more adolescent, some are like forceful adults, others like innocent children. Individuals might and then be thrown off course by surrounding situations into adolescent turmoil. The netherworld oligarchy is made up of forceful adults tossed into adolescent tantrums. We need to transform ourselves and our

46

collectives to be more like our original selves, before burdened by societal pressures, as children who seek to heal not harm.

The world spins on fear. If we had no fear we would behave differently. You can't have a revolution without knowing the generalities and specifics of the macrocosm and microcosm and without shedding fear. When institutions go unchallenged, when adolescent reactions take place, it is because of fear. We are afraid what happened before will happen again —all the time.

Within us the battle rages as the ego, the hyperactive mind, tries to enslave hyper-capable consciousness in the status quo usually by injecting persuasions based on fear and societal pressures. In pursuing any process of self-development, whether physical strength, learning a subject, or practicing meditation, there are always times when the master and slave battle to postpone development, to prevent facing and overcoming stagnating fear. The master and slave within is akin to restraint and development wrestling. When one cages oneself into a routine it is primarily because one does not want to face oneself and the past. Layers of psychological ticks prevent us from facing our own inner state, bureaucratic dogma prevents us from facing our collective state.

The nation state depiction of the master and slave can be clarified through looking at North Korea for example. It is one of the most overtly extreme institutions of master above all. A place where we have yet to see the slave confront the master, but it is nearly inevitable. One day, one thing will happen and it might be as little a thing as a misstep or misspoken arrangement or paranoia of a misstep and the next thing you know the nation has flipped, the slave is self-realized. The master could yield before confrontation, but when an institutional tree is as unforgiving as North Korea, there is little likelihood of that. The North Korean master does everything it can, often in the most overtly repressive manner, to prevent any revolution of individual and mass consciousness.

On the opposite end of the national spectrum, as opposed to the overt repression of North Korea, is the U.S.A. Originally founded on revolution, the

U.S.A. today is as afraid of revolution as any other institution under the master slave dynamic. The U.S.A. forms ways in which to prevent the revolutionaries in different ways. Instead of killing them before or after they revolt, in the U.S.A. the revolutionary drive is killed in the first place as is illustrated by the overall apathy in the Wendigo world, the culture of separation.

In the U.S.A. and in North Korea it's implied everything is discovered and everything is invented and we are at the pinnacle of development and there is no reason to question beyond how you can best serve the institution. In the U.S.A. there is the impetus to make new laws and new gadgets for old systems, but there is little invention and revolution outside of the design structure which works in, for, by and of the netherworld oligarchy. The system in the U.S.A. is a bit more refined and subtle and even though revolutionary culture is often confrontationally or underhandedly stopped it is mostly quelled before consideration through the dominant doomstruck apathy.

People can be distracted and lose focus to frivolous pursuits and selfish bucketlists. In North Korea there are no distractions to institutional dogma, in the U.S.A. there is every distraction. North Korea is a patriarchal godhead culture overtly preventing revolution. The U.S.A. is an entertainment war culture and though more open and tolerant of social revolution, revolution results in the same in both nations; attention of authorities. Always ask what is promoted, what is prohibited, by whom and for what reason.

Every battle between the master and slave, every revolution, every removal of an institutional tree, results in beasts of the field arriving clandestinely to influence, to slow or stop the movement or to infiltrate the movement to control it for various, nearly always, unscrupulous ends. When unscrupulous people seek an institutions falling, they usually want to find a way to get a cut. Revolutionary movements have to make sure they are not infiltrated. One way to do this is keep the message simple and make action direct.

The level of infiltration is normally only guessable as are the conspirators origins. But it is well documented that police, working for city governments, run by mayors, who had telephone conferences on how they would deal with the

OWS movement for instance, infiltrated the OWS movement. Normally infiltrations have institutional roots. The bigger the movement the more likely there are many infiltrators from multiple institutions. Revolutionary movements need qualifiers for participation to confirm they are not police or anarchists or police posing as anarchists.

When revolutions of the mind are brought to the streets and when institutional trees wither, when it's obvious the master and the slave are battling for control, others, whether vines already attached or invasive species, will attempt to sway the outcome of the battle upward. Usually they are supportive of the master and will directly or clandestinely subvert the slave, up until a point. When it is obvious there will be a new master or at least no more old master, they will support the slave. There are always other collaborators in the battle of the master and slave. There are confluences and synergistic connections which might attempt to transform revolution into a hailstorm of jumbled confrontation and jeopardous outcome.

The revolt of the slave against the master in Syria, 2012, which followed the largely peaceful fall of Egypt and confrontation in Libya, sprouted into a full blown war, where enlisted men, at the time of this release, fight against their own countrymen or institutionhood and conscripted soldiers from all over, interwoven with strategic interests of other national interests.

Masters of alternative institutions might instigate and assist the slave revolution against or assist the master confront the slave, or wait. Perhaps if President Assad reformed his ways the war would not have been. Revolution is bound to take place, war only if the institution is ardent about repressing it. Mikhail Gorbachev made reforms, but the Soviet Union fell anyway. However the transition took place peacefully.

The First Amendment is the real patriot act and it doesn't matter where one is located or what institution one is under for it to be effective. The recent Patriot Act and the institutions united decision lend individual rights to institutional trees, akin to what Jesus revolted against. And yet no matter how the Bill of Rights is chipped at, no matter how the overall ant-institutional sentiment of the Declaration of Independence is distorted and even if the First Amendment is outright eliminated, it will still be a prescription for peaceful revolution. Just as Jesus was a great revolutionary and an inspiration for revolution both inner and outer, both spiritually and secularly, the First Amendment is a great prescription for revolution. The First Amendment is in fact the only thing that makes the idea of American exceptionalism, besides Native American Indian ideas, valid.

If our First Amendment rights were eliminated today it would still present the formula to obtain and maintain the rights therein. No matter what happens, no matter where you are and no matter what institution you're under, the prescription and direction for liberty presented in the First Amendment is extremely powerful.

It's a new world, it's the netherworld oligarchy. And the specifics of the First Amendment have been misjudged, undervalued, misinterpreted and misrepresented. The complex world causes complex misunderstandings which fog movements, but the First Amendment remains valuable for it represents the humanistic pulse that cannot be ravaged by the vines on the tree. The First Amendment is a tangible prescription for revolution, of the construction and destruction of symbols. The First Amendment is a declaration of rights and a prescription to keep our rights. If the First Amendment is lost and eroded, if information is not open, society declines, even the culture of separation cannot thrive without the ideas in the First Amendment. Without it we would be led by oligarchical institutions to our demise.

Gluscabi is a transformational hero known throughout New England. After unsuccessfully hunting Gluscabi goes to his grandmother and tells her of his problem. His grandmother makes him a magical game bag which can hold all the animals he can put into it. Gluscabi goes back into the forest and tells all the creatures that the world is ending and that he has made a new world where they will be safe and the bag is the entrance to the new world. The terrified animals jump into the magical game bag and soon Gluscabi has all the animals of the world. He happily returns to the village pleased he will never have to hunt again. He shows his grandmother who is very disappointed. She informs him animals cannot live in a game bag and asks him what his grandchildren will eat. Gluscabi understands and Gluscabi the animals to the forest telling them he prevented the calamity.

Without the First Amendment how will the grandmothers speak and inform the youth caught up in a Wendigo world of the illmindedness? Without the First Amendment who will speak for our grandchildren?

The Time Is Now

It is time to put love, locals, land and liberty above institutions, ideals and income. Your nation, your religion is a great, but that does not mean there are not equally great places or beliefs with alternate greatness. Institutional jingoism is spurred by the unconscious and results in a culture of separation invariably causing people to ignore the big picture, riding with blinders on so as to see what we want to see.

If people took a look at the cityscape instead of the city block, if people shed the blinders of institutional trust we could see we are not being told the truth. Most individuals simply need a reference and they'll believe anything and eventually the majority tends to fall in line. Instead of believing what we're told we should believe what we comprehend. Institutions tell individuals to obey while they degrade the human situation and the very biological balance of Earth Mother. Institutions convince us it's okay as they extract all they can and leave nothing. The First Amendment enables us to question and criticize institutions openly, loudly and vulgarly if necessary. We can proudly say the sensible or the profane or a combination of the two, like fuck the devils running the military industrial complex profiting from killing. Fuck the prison industrial complex, because they profit from imprisoning people, half of them often for drugs and half of them for marijuana. And fuck accurate statistics when hearts are jailed so others cash in, the point is the point, not facts, not f-acts. Fuck the facts and how they twist them. Fuck the chemical and petrolithic agricultural toxins genetically modified seed is made to grow in. Fuck Monsanto, DuPont, Dow and GE. And fuck the facts, how they made them to be. To do anything other than the right thing requires arrangement of facts. Doing the right thing requires no facts, nothing but the heart.

"Certain things catch your eye, but pursue only those that capture your heart."
~American Indian proverb of unknown origin

Fuck all the institutions, straight up, the longer they've been around the worse they are. They are motivated to profit in a society that kills and jails and to maintain the status quo that kills and jails. Fuck al the institutions, they mean nothing next to Earth Mother.

The First Amendment is first because of its exceptionalism, the rarity of the rights among institutions. The First Amendment is the real patriot act. The more recent Patriot Act promotes proactive interrogation, surveillance and expansion of the military and prison industrial complex. The Citizens United, or more accurately institutions united Supreme Court decision removed corporate campaign spending limitations, effectively making it so that billionaires could bankroll politicians, as was demonstratively the case during the 2012 Republican presidential primaries. The First Amendment should is meant to be applicable to individuals, but institutions adopted it.

Good drugs were made contraband and replaced with dangerous prescriptions, which can cause physical and mental turmoil. Contraband results in the buildup of a prison system and violent enterprises which thrive off of contraband profit. Contraband results in a world so screwed up that people risk time just to get a buzz and step outside the day to day reality of the netherworld oligarchy for a moment.

Fuck the corporate charlatans impeding our right to have clean air, water, and nutritious food so that they can become netherworld oligarchical masters. The First Amendment allows me to produce a painting or poem decrying the netherworld oligarchy to the Nth degree. Reality has been paved over, but there is no denying it, eventually the truth surfaces no matter how we all want the truth to be one way or another. The whole world likes to believe that we are developing, but we are not even sustainable. The more you realize it the more expletives are necessary to decry it.

The First Amendment defines rights and prescribes the way to take action against wrongdoing perpetuated by institutions. Many nations today do not allow free expression, most in the past did not and it seems all institutions increasingly tolerate less of it, even here in the U.S.A. Well, fuck them. Stand up and say, 'I love you, I understand you, but fuck you for being/doing/enacting/perpetuating the corruption of...' and then insert whatever the proper specific usurpation suits as eloquently and succinctly as possible. There comes a time...

In my experience a hearty fuck you at the right time in the wrong place usually shuts everybody up and shocks everybody for just long enough for eloquence to take over the silence. Few will interrupt your peppered reasoning and those who do can be shut down. A polite 'fuck you' followed by intelligent reasoning usually makes everything else roll off the tongue comparatively easy as well.

The political punk music group Pussy Riot in Russia performed a protest song about and spurred by state and church collectivism in early 2012. Three women were sentenced to two years each in Russian Gulags for hooliganism. The song they performed which caused institutional repression is called Mother of God Drive Putin Away. Other tracks they produced include, Death to Prison Freedom to Protests, Putin Pissed Himself and Putin Lights Up The Fires.

In 2004, after producing the ten minute film entitled Submission, Theo Van Gogh was assassinated by an offended Muslim. The film is about violence against women in Muslim societies. The idea enflamed the Muslim community and he was killed because of his creation. The builders and destroyers of symbols create and no matter if rock song or documentary the creation will sound like fuck you to someone. So one should come right out and say it, no matter what. Fuck close minded national religious zealots who would hurt or kill any of god's creatures for any claimed godly reason, especially an artist for creating something questioning wrongdoing.

Whatever the artistic creation, The First Amendment is a sort of litmus test of cultural development and understanding. Normally the amount of freedom of political expression, especially as it concerns the oligarchical collectivism of church and state, corresponds to how well women are treated in a society. Repression of expression and women go hand in hand all over the world. The more open and tolerant of expression people are, the more developed they are and the less violent they are to women and otherwise.

When institutions or individuals react against critical art, you know there is something wrong with the status quo. You can infer that the powers that be find the information or perspective a threat to the status quo they control and make gains from. And they employ emotional ticks among their supporters so that when Catholic Church pedophilia or Israeli persecution of Palestinians or the corruption of their favorite corporation is mentioned they are angered. The First Amendment allows for freedom of religion, freedom to question religion and freedom to mock religion, it is the freedom for and from religion and freedom from any oligarchical collectivism of church and state. The First Amendment enables freedom of religion and not-so coincidentally the freedom to assemble in protest, as well as the freedom to write about anything or create any art, in protest of religion or otherwise. You can't have freedom with exceptions.

The ability for a minority within a group to practice free expression is as qualitative a measure of a society's maturity as is their treatment of women. The extent to which such people are repressed is measure of how developed a collective is. The more open to women and expression the more artistic and better their creations. The more repressive and easily offended a group is the more juvenile the expressions will likely be.

The First Amendment is liberating. If the whole world was guaranteed First Amendment rights we would be in an open paradise where no one could be hurt for speaking out against abuse or corruption and no one would face consequences for artistic expression.

The First Amendment allows promotion of political and religious beliefs and guarantees the right of the artist to produce anything and the reporter to say anything. Sensational art spurs societal progression, instigation of new questioning develops new thinking. Sometimes the best art is offensive and sometimes the most offensive art is only popular at all because of those who take offense. Art provokes thought.

Human history is the story of the interaction of individuals with institutions. The history of the individual is one of development and stagnation, of peaks and valleys. At times we have elevated consciousness while other times we have sunk, as if stuck on the rope over a chasm between animal and uberman. Individuals have developed and mass consciousness has developed too. Societal progression starts with the individual and expands to groups, then communities, then regions and then the world.

Modern history provides audio and video recordings of the Civil Rights movement. One can see in this peaceful movement the irrefutable evidence for the power of one individual reverberating and changing communities in Alabama and then the South and then the entire U.S.A and ultimately the world. The apartheid in South Africa eventually fell, perhaps traceable to someone in Alabama essentially refusing to move and questioning racism. All revolutions require is development of consciousness.

Rosa Parks rattled the status quo in Montgomery making herself a symbol, under racial oppression. Sometimes you don't have to stand up to make a stand, sometimes you just have to know something is wrong and do something, anything. Rosa Parks was by no means physically helpless; but she was a small woman armed only with strong conviction and clear intention. She peacefully refused to participate in a very artistic and concrete way.

Rosa Parks sat down and brought attention to a mandated, officially sanctioned, racial wrong. She enacted the power of one in defiance and ceased participation in exploitation. The Montgomery Bus Boycott ensued her rule breaking and eventually the discrimination was eliminated.

The netherworld oligarchy of institutions over individuals is more of the same with the occasional never seen before. Oligarchies are nothing new and about as old as civilization itself. Revolution against them is nearly as old and practically inevitable, resulting in intolerant and repressive institutions and revolution, the building and destruction of symbols, not necessarily violence. It's up to the reactions to demands for change. King George III and the related oligarchical institutions reacted repressively after the Boston Tea Party, eventually resulting in war. The appeasement of the will of the people, like in Montgomery and the Civil Rights movement as a whole, exemplifies nonviolent revolution. The institutions decide if revolution will be nonviolent or not by their reactions.

No matter location or time period, institutions operate via rhetoric and formality, whereas individuals operate on truth and reality. These institutional formalities tend to infiltrate the thinking of society. There is no way we can understand history or the present without being able to extrapolate and understand formality and truth and how the distinctions are blurred to steer thinking. Without understanding the distinction between formality and reality we will never understand politics, society or even scientific studies.

One way to understand the difference between formality and truth is through examination of scientific studies another is to look at current events in depth and then see how news programs presents them. Through examination of scientific studies one see the formality and the truth, the institutionalization and the indigenous and genuine. Everyone eats and everyone is subject to government decisions on our food. The new implementation of vast amounts of pesticides, herbicides and fertilizers is called 'conventional' food production. A 'scientific' study comparing conventionally grown food with organically grown food concluded that there was no distinguishable difference between conventional and organic. Scientific studies present their findings as to what they consider the truth, but you have dig to find the perimeters for the conclusions. What foods were involved in the study? Some foods do not require massive amounts of toxins to grow conventionally. What nutrients were measured? What toxins were measured? Where were the foods sourced? Were genetically modified foods included in the test? The truth is no matter what formality one abides by poisons reveal themselves. Nobody knows the long term implications of genetically modified organisms as foods grown with franchise toxins. The formality is there is no difference between GMO food grown with pesticides, the truth is organic is the real convention of millennia and is more nutritious, less toxic and tends to taste better than corporicultural products.

Those with an aversion to politics are averse to contemplating the entirety of reality for all interaction is influenced by politics. Politics, perhaps because of those averse to it, shapes individuals more than individuals shape politics. Understanding politics enables evaluation and elevation of self and surroundings.

Understanding the difference between formality and truth, between rhetoric and reality is itself a measure of mental adulthood. The more one obfuscates reality and revels in formality the more infantile one likely is. Those who shed truth and adopt formality normally have some selfish reason to do so. Examples of this can be seen in the operation of most any institution where people forgo the real, for the presented deal. The divine right of kings in Europe is an extreme of this, but any leniency to institutions in such uplifts formality over truth. The Citizen's United Supreme Court decision similarly yields to formality by allowing wealth to have more power in political discourse. It's another example of truth, of individual rights being shed in favor of formality, of institutions. You can say corporations are people all you want, the fact is institutions are not individuals.

There is barely rarely truth in formality and reality never ever requires it. The truth is that history is a story of the interaction between individuals and institutions. The truth is human history itself is a history of politics, but it is also history of the human mind.

"Men by their constitutions are naturally divided into two parties: 1. Those who fear and distrust the people, and wish to draw all powers from them into the hands of the higher classes. 2. Those who identify themselves with the people, have confidence in them, cherish and consider them as the most honest and safe, although not the most wise depositary of the public interests. In every country these two parties exist, and in every one where they are free to think, speak, and write, they will declare themselves. Call them, therefore, Liberals and Serviles, Jacobins and Ultras, Whigs and Tories, Republicans and Federalists, Aristocrats and Democrats, or by whatever name you please, they are the same parties still and pursue the same object. The last one of Aristocrats and Democrats is the true one expressing the essence of all." ~Thomas Jefferson to Henry Lee, 1824.

Label them however you like, but most are aristocrat or democrat, master or slave, institutionalized or indigenous, authoritarian or libertarian. And now, in the postmodern netherworld oligarchy of environmental decay, after a century of the petrolithic era, after close to a century the global nuclear experiment we are all complicit or complacent to the destruction of Earth Mother.

In the U.S.A. "All men are created equal." Of course we know some people are better equipped to be runners, some need glasses and some can do amazing feats of mind and body. All people are equal in that we are all equally improvable and we all have equal rights. Human beings were not made physically or mentally equal, but we are all equals and should accept each other as equals. One of the greatest philosophers ever known believed that all people are born equally good. Socrates announced that all men are good and all are only tricked into doing wrong. When you don't question you are easily tricked into wrongdoing.

Hatred is learned and it is used amongst all sides of a war to enable destruction. During World War One both sides believed they were fighting for liberty and that the others were evil to enable the killing. Today hatred is used just as it was in all wars and in the fictional 1984 to stagnate society and keep our minds closed. Hatred results in close-mindedness and being closed to our potential.

Buddha taught compassion and became and enlightened being meditating on it. Compassion is the opposite of hate and has the opposite effect on our body, mind, spirit and surroundings. Hatred allows us all to be tricked into being blind to the brotherhood of man. Hatred allows institutions to promote war. Hatred leads to closed mindedness and closes one off to healing spiritual energy and/or god. The reason many spiritual or energetic practices will not allow certain people to learn the certain things is because our energy is closed, blocked off and littered with hatred, so much of it we sometimes don't realize it's there. And so much of it that only slow introduction can be safely processed. Hatred removes goodness and instills pain, compassion removes pain and offers happiness.

There is no way to reap the reward of spiritual energy if you are closed off and have hatred. There is no way to begin to heal yourself and surroundings with hatred for god's creatures on different paths. If you are inspired by hatred you have been tricked to think that way to serve institutions. The only way to be open to energy, the only way to be open-minded is to be completely open to compassion and forgiveness. That does not mean to accept foolishness or violence, but accept that everyone of god's creatures is on a path of ascension and we were all fools at least once and perhaps many times and we are capable of being fooled at any time and becoming better beings. Esoterically compassion leads to open access to energy. Exoterically compassion makes it so we cannot be fooled into taking action on behalf of violent or exploitive institutions promoting hatred.

The idea that people only do wrong if they are ignorant of it or tricked into it is considered to be the flaw of Socrates. Socrates was such a great philosopher that he had only one flaw: he believed man was good. The flaw may well be in people suggesting Socrates was wrong. The culture of separation assumes we are born bad and must be trained and controlled with a police state.

That all men are good and simply tricked to do wrong is hardly based on wishful thinking, but actually a highly astute observation. People are tricked into wrongdoing, often on behalf of institutions. Not everyone who does wrong will admit it's for an institution or because they have been steered, because they were tricked. One of the greatest tricks, the societal flaw, is that people think we need to be controlled otherwise we'll do wrong. The unaccepted Socratic profundity actually reveals the flaw of conventional thinking. Socrates believed people should be given opportunity to do right. The status quo of the netherworld oligarchy corrals people to do no wrong. It is the difference between the institutionalization of the sophist and the individuation of the Socratic.

Have you ever looked at a river that once was pure, a mountain lake that was once clear, an ocean that was once thriving, inhaled air that was once fresh and looked over forests once dear and asked why? Why do I live in a dysfunctional society? Then you're probably on the right path. Those in the culture of separation never question such let alone construct or destroy symbols of any sort. Most people do not consider the fact the environment was once cleaner. All bodies of water and every breath of air was once clearer. Everything you eat and touch has been polluted so that a few people could become wealthy beyond belief and this will be true for generations. The netherworld oligarchy is turning everyone into indentured servants to phantom entities. The environmental catastrophes, Chernobyl, Hanford and Fukushima among the most severe, will cost Earth Mother forever and only a few people benefitted for a brief time, if at all. That's the calamity of the netherworld oligarchy.

If you've ever been among those who question you've probably been near drowned by waves of conformity. Feeling upset in upsetting surroundings is more reasonable than ignoring or joining in upsetting things. Questioning and stepping out of line defines leadership and leads to solutions, however it calls attention to the upsetting surroundings potentially upsetting people about the alert for the first time. In the netherworld oligarchy and it is perfectly normal to feel upset. In fact those who do not feel upset in the have been indoctrinated dangerously to ignore dire circumstances. Feeling lost is sometimes the only way to find your way. Otherwise people just continue toward the cliff edge, not admitting or adjusting. Feeling lost is a gift and is indicative one has managed to retain some sense of individuality and compassionate humanity despite the netherworld oligarchy.

Perhaps the first global transformation was arranged through global colonialism instigated by violent and exploitive European institutions. These institutions of chartered companies explored and stole the Americas, much of Africa and much of Asia. From then on globalization has expanded and localization has been belittled. These chartered companies drew many of the national borders and interests we individuals deal with today.

The worst aspect of globalization is enslavement of individuals in order to exploit resources. Tea was the commodity to represent such exploitation at the Boston Tea Party. Today any number of commodities could be used to represent exploitation. GMO corn is symbolic of the institutional takeover of today. Corn is a sacred food of all American Indians and now it ultimately has been stolen too, just like their land and language. Feeling lost leads to finding our way. Being exploited led to building counters to the colonizing European institutions. The U.S.A. was founded on countering oligarchical globalization. The Declaration of Independence is proof of as much, despite the inevitable institutional steering to the netherworld oligarchy, beginning with the exile and murder of American Indians.

The Boston Tea Party went against the institutions of exploitation and globalization. It was an act of defiance and was a catalyst for independence and eventual similar defiance toward independence, led by Gandhi. In Colonial America it was tea, in India Gandhi used salt. Gandhi marched hundreds of miles to the sea to illegally harvest the plentiful sea salt and inspired others to do so with him. The symbols used were different, but the defiance of exploitation is the same. One has to feel lost before finding one's way and one has to feel one is being led the wrong way to stop and defy the progression.

Colonialism has led to increased globalization and institutionalization and has decreased localization and individuation. Today other resources are used to exploit people, but like tea or salt or petrol or palm the format is the same, only in the netherworld oligarchy the effects are an order of magnitude greater than previously imaginable.

Humanity has saturated the environment and changed it, in ways we cannot completely fathom and in ways that are completely obvious. The first physical inundation was through the global burning and use of petroleum products layering the whole planet with toxins and poisons. The petrolithic era is the planetary age of oil and war and war for oil. Since World War One it's been planetary pollution and obliteration, war enabling use of oil and oil fueling war in an endless cycle.

In World War Two humanity spawned another physically measurable era. In 1942 the nuclear era began with the bombing of New Mexico and then cities in Japan. Both of these energy and war systems initiated new planetary eras of perspective and physicality. The main reason these systems exist is because of war, the main reason they continue to be prominent is because of the oligarchy. Petrol and nuclear are not the best sources of fuel, they are the best sources of fuel for war and they are the best fuels for the netherworld oligarchy.

"How smooth must be the language of the whites, when they can make right look like wrong, and wrong like right." ~Black Hawk

The worldwide burning of petrol and nuclear material has released pollution of incalculable amounts, altering and destroying life in incalculable ways. The components of oil, coal, natural gas and nuclear experimentation are in our blood, our bones and everything. The background levels of radiation in the world, especially in the Northern Hemisphere, are on a steady uptick. The biggest nuclear facilty in the world, home to six nuclear reactors, is a total failure and calamity marking time like A.D. and will continue to pollute the Pacific Ocean and world forever.

The petrolithic and nuclear eras have led to drastic climate change or more accurately enhanced planetary entropy or global environmental destruction. Both the systems work through extraction of earthbound substances, costly refinement and oligarchical delivery systems. It is misleading to differentiate the two, nuclear being labeled alternative to petrol, suggesting it is more environmentally safe. Both systems are controlled by a few, benefit a few, are subsidized directly and indirectly in order to make economically viable and both endanger the ecosystem to the point of causing extinction level events. Petroleum and nuclear energy are the longest Wendigo claws.

The debate over global warming and the conspiracies therein, on all sides of the argument, is moot. The argument over global warming, the conspiracies and cover-ups are all just distractions, global warming itself is a distraction. The real debate should be on how to stop global environmental destruction. Every strata of Earth is negatively impacted by the global burning of petrol and nuclear fuels, the guts of Earth Mother. There is no debate on the catastrophic destruction of the Wendigo claws, the pollution of all elements.

The debate is on the ever fluctuation of temperature, not the increasing destruction of the atmosphere and oceans. All water is negatively altered to the point much of is undrinkable and uninhabitable. Everything is polluted on a scale never before experienced. The real debate should be on clean air and pure water. The debate on global warming is a distraction to the real debate; what to do about the culture of separation causing global environmental destruction.

Individuals and collectives have mostly existed in cooperation with their environment. On the occasion they did not, they moved or perished. Indigenous behavior cooperated with the land and surrounding resources. The petrolithic and nuclear institutions are designed with unsustainable infrastructure to feed the Wendigo whose hunger is infinite and whose concern for others and the future is nonexistent.

Rudolf Diesel designed the Diesel engine with localization in mind. The Diesel engine was meant to be fueled by locally sourced bio-fuels to power local industry. Hemp is the oiliest plant and one of the easiest to grow. Petrol was a secondary, dirty option. Individual/agricultural production and facilitation of fuel is not nearly as wild an idea as the typical oligarchical extraction processes. Rudolf Diesel did not conceive oligarchical control of the extraction and distribution of petroleum, but imagined locally sourced biofuel.

Institutions seek to globalize and homogenize. Individuals seek to localize and specialize. The netherworld oligarchy, formed like a pyramid costs entirely. A very few prosper at the cost of the micro and macro, the individual and the environment. Even if you don't use petrol it costs you and your surroundings, even if you don't benefit from nuclear experimentation, you pay.

After the land theft and removal of sovereign rule that the Native American Indians suffered, it was learned some reservations they were forced onto had major mineralogical deposits. Further theft occurred and regional environmental destruction in mining for minerals like gold and later uranium on the reservations. Everything was taken away from the American Indian peoples, in gradual form. Today open uranium mines in Arizona on Navajo land and in the Black Hills on Sioux land leak massive amounts of radiation constantly. Nuclear experimentation destroys through the first phase of extraction before processing and burning. Today, we are all on the rez, and our liberties are diluted in steps.

Nuclear experimentation multiplies the oligarchical madness of the petrolithic era a thousand fold. The many are dependent on the few for their energy, but the system which profits the few in the area, endangers the entire surrounding population and ultimately the planet. Nuclear experimentation endangers us all directly and catastrophically. Everyone and everything on the planet contains manmade radioactive elements dispersed in the known and unknown nuclear disasters, the extraction process, power generation and detonation experimentation. The Fukushima and Chernobyl nuclear accidents alone contaminated and still contaminate the whole planet. Add two thousand and some odd detonations underground, underwater and in the air, plus the inevitable accidents such as the one that took place at W.I.P.P. in New Mexico, and you have the netherworld oligarchy where we'll be paying for the lobster parties of nuclear corporations and nuclear nations forever.

There is another paradigm shift that occurred recently, another change so dramatic as to constitute a new era. It is however merely cultural and not physically detectable. It is the era of information achieved through technological advancements. The information era began with the growth of the internet and the advancement of communication technology.

There is fourth paradigm recently catapulted us into another concurrent social era. The era of institutionalization, like the information era, did not begin overnight. Just like technology had to develop to accommodate the era of information, legislation had to develop to make way for the era of institutionalization now cementing the netherworld oligarchy. The legislation to finalize the era of institutionalization was the Citizen's United Supreme Court decision to allow unlimited campaign funding for advertising from corporate entities or anyone.

The Declaration of Independence is the most rebellious document ever produced. It is a fuck you letter of the highest order. It states the reasoning for the Colonies discontinuance of support. It inspired a loose knit group of people to refuse to obey the exploitive royal European institutions. One could say this was the beginning of the era of individualization. The institutions united (Citizen's United) Supreme Court decision ended this era, however it was a gradual process of course.

The Colonies realized their Declaration would result in an uncertain future. They fought to counter to the predominant oligarchical institutionalization because it was wrong for individualization. Nothing was certain, but there comes a tipping point when the usurpations of institutions become too much and laws are broken for civil disobedience. The Declaration of Independence, The Bill of Rights and the sentiment behind much of the Constitution is based on countering institutions. Since the nation's inception there have been many instances of oligarchical exploitation, slavery and the obliteration of Native peoples, the U.S.A. is still based on countering the oligarchical institutionalization of the world.

The Declaration of Independence declared from institutional domination of English royalty, parliament and the British East India Company. The Company John and similar colonial operations like Dutch East India Company were the first global institutions and if not for the Revolutionary War, would have likely initiated the beginning of the era of institutionalization. Because of the Revolutionary War the era of institutionalization slowly progressed. The era of institutionalization was long in the making. It did not suddenly transform, it was slowly magnified to the global proportions of today. The Revolutionary War cast off the blood right of kings, extolling unlimited rights to families and any confusion between individual and institution as exhibited in the calling the B.E.I.C. The Company John. The institutions united decision removed the last vestige of individual power. Up until then there was a chance that the individual might have an impact. Now the era of institutionalization is effectively a worldwide phenomenon. Now any institutions or individual can provide unlimited funding to a political candidate in the U.S.A.

All profits and heroes have always promoted the idea of individuation. While all corporate/government collectives have always institutionalized people to the point they willingly sacrifice themselves in the name of the oligarchy. The era of institutionalization has been built up to where it is today. Decisions and laws were inserted into the collective mindset in the U.S.A. beginning with the Supreme Court Southern Pacific railroad decision of 1886, in favor of the railroad company over the individual landowner. The era of institutionalization expanded with hemp/cannabis prohibition as a means to favor industry over agriculture, large scale forestry instead of hemp farming, putting institutions over individuals. It expanded into the entire war on drugs and the prison industrial complex. Medicinal prohibition enhances institutionalization with allopathic insurance mandates posing as access to individual healthcare. If individuals were favored over institutions the world would be a lot different, healthcare would be a lot different. As it is institutions are put before and above individuals.

"Before our white brothers arrived to make us civilized men, we didn't have any kind of prison. Because of this, we had no delinquents. Without a prison, there can be no delinquents. We had no locks nor keys and therefore among us there were no thieves. When someone was so poor that he couldn't afford a horse, a tent or a blanket, he would, in that case, receive it all as a gift. We were too uncivilized to give great importance to private property. We didn't know any kind of money and consequently, the value of a human being was not determined by his wealth. We had no written laws laid down, no lawyers, no politicians, therefore we were not able to cheat and swindle one another. We were really in bad shape before the white men arrived and I don't know how to explain how we were able to manage without these fundamental things that (so they tell us) are so necessary for a civilized society."

~John (Fire) Lame Deer

Individuation has been subverted and replaced with institutionalization and with Citizen's United Supreme Court opinion the era of institutionalization is ubiquitous. In 2012 corporate sponsors injected so much money into the Republican primary that each candidate stuck around almost to the end resulting in lack of consideration for Ron Paul and Mitt Romney becoming the Republican candidate.

The great philosophers and theologians in the world all note that defiance against oligarchical institutions is profound and also leads to profundity. Revolutionary ideas mean nothing until they make money. The measure of profit is often the only measure at all. Nietzsche noted crossing the chasm, Hegel noted the master refusing to obey the master, Jesus tossed tables, Gandhi refused to obey peacefully. It is the duty of mankind to stand up and confront oligarchies. The error of institutions began sometime 10,000 years ago, when society formed pyramidal caste constructs, but many societies offered different visions. Basically wherever matriarchal society was favored there was peace, patriarchal society offered war. The error of institutions has been ongoing for millennia with the belittling of peaceful feminine rule, the era of institutionalization, the near total global institutionalization, began on March, 24, 2009.

The Citizen's United decision enables the institutional control. Citizen's United is a political action committee that campaigns for legislation and election. The Citizen United decision allows unlimited corporate and union funding of political action committees.

The Supreme Court put institutional sovereignty above or on par with the rights of individuals. Just before the institutions united decision the Patriot Act swung in, as if on a vine from an institutional branch, prepared before 9/11 and in response to 9/11. The Patriot Act made it so government/corporate collectives could track individuals, removing individual rights from individuals and lending them to institutions. The institutions united decision made it so money talks and the larger the amount you possess the louder the voice you have. The institutionalization progressed in tolerable steps since the 1886 court 'opinion.'

"At bottom, the Court's opinion is thus a rejection of the common sense of the American people, who have recognized a need to prevent corporations from undermining self-government since the founding, and who have fought against the distinctive corrupting potential of corporate electioneering since the days of Theodore Roosevelt. It is a strange time to repudiate that common sense. While American democracy is imperfect, few outside the majority of this Court would have thought its flaws included a dearth of corporate money in politics."

Justice Stevens, Dissenting opinion on institutions united

Strange times indeed, Orwellian in fact. Industry has been supplanted over agriculture since September 29, 1913, the day Diesel died. Promotion of war machines and war profit has been the status quo since, magnified with the inception of the nuclear era. Another major stepping stone along the path to the era of institutionalization is the international drug war. Individuals are locked down left and right for narcotics. Nuclear experimentation is arguably the most dangerous undertaking imaginable and it is legal, it is subsidized and promoted by national institutions worldwide. Marijuana and hemp especially are a danger to no one whereas nuclear experimentation is a danger to all life. Drugs are supposed to be dangerous, but hemp and marijuana are more productive than dangerous. And nuclear experimentation is supposed to be productive, but it's dangerous. The reason for promotion of one and prohibition of the other is that one uplifts individuals and the other uplifts institutions.

If petrolithic and nuclear mineralogical dependence was slowed and hemp was sown localization could take root instead of globalization, the opposite of global environmental destruction. Hemp is the oiliest plant on the planet. But today the source of food, fuel and medicine that is hemp/cannabis is prohibited and nuclear experimentation is promoted. Today there is environmentally destructive institutionalization and reduced individuation, the netherworld oligarchy.

Individuation, coined by Carl Gustav Jung, is the process of becoming a conscious individual. Conscious individuals would never allow institutions to rule a Wendigo world. Conscious individuals would never accept a donut in exchange for their self-rule. Only those unaware of self and surroundings living in a culture of separation would be subject to institutionalization without question. The development of consciousness is the best way to potentiate individuals and collectives.

Welcome to the era of institutionalization, the postmodern netherworld oligarchy, where institutions have renewed the blood right of kings, where institutions are allowed to exploit individuals. This is nothing new of course. It's always been individuals versus institutions, liberty versus authority. This duo dances in every revolution.

"The real division is not between conservatives and revolutionaries but between authoritarians and libertarians." ~George Orwell

The degraded and polluted Earth Mother and the enhanced technological capability of institutions (in preventing revolution) is new. Revolution in the petrolithic era, the nuclear era, the era of information and the era of institutionalization, the netherworld oligarchy populated by Wendigos requires peaceable means. Peaceful revolution is the only way a revolution can work in the netherworld oligarchy for so much of the status quo is based on war and so much of the institutional infrastructure is based on eliminating and preventing it.

The militaristic idea of Mutually Assured Destruction, that we build nuclear weaponry to prevent war degrades life even if it manages to prevent war. In the Wendigo world technology could be used to uplift all peoples, but it is used for ideas like M.A.D. and to institute Orwellian surveillance. Nuclear experimentation quells revolution and keeps hold of the war state, just as much as it does prevent war. The military agenda is highly influential. Peaceable revolution is possible and is the only way to save and advance humanity. The only problem in winning peaceful revolution is starting it. People are trained to maintain tolerance and allow institutional abominations like M.A.D. and global nuclear experimentation and further scorn the protesters of such systems.

There are five primary colors of individuation, five rights of revolution. Like five fingers each works on its own and come together to perform unlimited tasks including wrestling Wendigos. Just as notes together make music, flavors make taste, and colors make paintings, the five rights of revolution makeup activism and individuation. And just like music and color permeate silence and emptiness, individuation permeates the emptiness of institutionalization in the netherworld oligarchy. There is no silence with music. And in the same way liberty eliminates empty institutionalization. Institutions are not individuals, my friend.

The application of human rights to inhuman institutions leads to institutional exploitation of individuals. The United States of America was founded on revolution. Revolution and evolution do not have to be violent; in fact anything revolutionary today has to be nonviolent. For violence is normal, part of the status quo everywhere. The purveyors of violence, the military industrial complex, created the internet as a means of communication after a nuclear war. The internet is a result of the military industrial complex, an invention spawned out of the potential necessity to communicate after nuclear war. Politics influences directly and indirectly. Today individuals can utilize the tools of war to communicate and prevent war. Revolution works like that. Often those in opposition of institutionalization think of themselves as patriots, instead let's be matriots in complete peaceful opposition to the masculine institutionalization.

War is stagnant destruction, revolution is change. Violence is the common denominator of the status quo. Therefore violence is not revolutionary and revolution is not violence. Revolution simply means turn, change. The change might happen rapidly, or might be slowed, but revolution is change and war is war. Being antiestablishment and revolutionary means being peaceful, as the establishment of the status quo for the last couple of thousand years is based on extreme institutional violence.

Technological revolution and societal revolution induce great change and yet, might slide through history without bloodshed. The Berlin Wall came down in a celebration without blood and fire. Gandhi freed South Asia from colonial rule in peace. The civil rights movement was a peaceful one. The Boston Tea Party was civil disobedience and peaceful protest, even though property was destroyed. If you have aggression, take it out on a symbolic wall, not people. Destroying something that might be used by individuals is terroristic, destroying the symbol a wall is nonviolent revolutionary activism, civil disobedience. Hurting a living being is violent and condemnable. Peaceful resistance and peaceful construction and destruction of symbols is revolutionary. Peace is requirement for revolution today. I do not suggest people relinquish their right to self-defense only to note that doing such is exemplified by many if not all great revolutionaries.

This is the essence of liberty: all people deserve respect and equality. And here is the catch; so long as their actions do no harm. If harm results their freedom must be restricted. If harm results freedom is rescinded. There are many complexities to this notion, but there are certain actions which cause no harm and therefore are totally open and free subjects or should be. And there are certain actions which cause great and broad harm and should be illegal and ceased, but are not.

The freedom of speech is the perfect illustration to this notion. One may say whatever one wants, unless it is harmful to others. One is not free to cause panic by yelling 'fire!' in a crowded theatre the metaphor goes. However one is free to ask if there is a fire in the theatre. And one should be free to yell at all authorities which repress people from putting out the fire institutions set.

There are many ways to accomplish change, progression, revolution or evolution through these measures. The specific order and concentration of the five rights of revolution should be left up to individual conditions, based simply on observations of actuality and pursuance of liberty.

Normally the five phases of revolution follow in the order presented. Normally the first part of the First Amendment, the freedom to question all things great and small, including the government the interpretation of god is first. The Boston Tea Party presents an archetypal story or revolution, of construction and destruction of symbols. No matter how the First Amendment has been co-opted, construed and criticized, no matter how it might be restricted, it is the prescription for activism. Those who participated in the Boston Tea Party conducted it in a peaceful manner to make a statement, to destroy a symbol. Many were prominent members of the community dressed as American Indians. Their garb was part of their statement and not disguise. They were renouncing the European oligarchies and symbolically adopting American Indian values. The American Indian dress was symbolic of their belonging, they were Americans now. The Boston Tea Party was defiant, but it was nonviolent. No one was hurt save a few who were made to run a gauntlet for attempting to pocket tea and degrade the symbolic destruction into theft.

First they questioned the institutional exploitation. Next they communicated and confirmed exploitation. Then they spoke out publicly about the exploitation. Following speaking out, they stopped their participation and boycotted the tea. Finally, when all else failed, the original patriots acted out of a redress of grievances and tossed The Company tea into Boston Harbor in a peaceful destruction of symbols.

The same formula used at the Boston Tea Party was used by Gandhi in his peaceful fight for liberty beginning with his famous salt march. Martin Luther King Jr. used the ideas too for individual empowerment, to further expand liberty in the U.S.A.

The five cardinal points for individual empowerment are so important a formula among institutionalization that they are assembled together as the first right, in one of first documents of its kind. The First Amendment presents the prescription to the five rights of revolution, the rest of the Bill of Rights backs it up. The First Amendment guarantees rights and also provides the prescription for activism, it alone validates modern American exceptionalism; the rights of revolution. The First Amendment is the formula for peaceful individual empowerment. It is as American as apple pie and is equally globally sourced and globally applicable. As an Amendment it protects the rights specifically, as a unification of the five cardinal points it is a prescription to keep them, to enact individual empowerment among oligarchical institutions. The First Amendment is an amalgamation of rights because they all pertain to the mutual concept of revolution and righteous rebellion. The First Amendment is an indication of secured rights, but also a directive of the fundamentals to individual empowerment under oligarchical institutions. The First Amendment provides individuals with rights and also direction on how to keep rights among institutions the likes of the British East India Corporation or British Petroleum that insist they have the rights of man.

The First Amendment presents the step-by-step course of action for individuals to keep their liberty. The following nine Amendments are further assurances that institutions respect individuals, but the First Amendment provides the course of action to secure and maintain individual liberty among oligarchical institutions. It presents the formula to construct and destroy symbols to elevate mass consciousness.

Since 9/11 and the Patriot Act the Writ of Habeas Corpus -the freedom of movement, association and speech- has fallen by the wayside like so much boxed tea in Boston Harbor. The Writ of Habeas Corpus was a specific response to institutional "abusive detention of persons without authority." The English Parliament adopted the Habeas Corpus Act in 1679, rooted in older laws, the critical individual right was adopted by the U.S.A. too. It provides individuals the right and opportunity to stand up to the institutions in court.

The Writ of Habeas Corpus specifies the time frame, that upon arrest, one must be arraigned, charged, held over for trial or dismissed, and tried by a jury of one's peers. Without Habeas Corpus individuals might be jailed indefinitely without reason and without ability to be heard or seen. The U.S.A. Constitution states: Habeas Corpus shall not be suspended unless in cases of rebellion and invasion, the public safety may require it. The first time Habeas Corpus was suspended in the U.S.A. was by Abraham Lincoln during the Civil War and the Reconstruction period. George Bush Jr. suspended the right after 9/11 and it remains so today. In 2006 the Military Commissions Act was passed determining that Habeas Corpus was not applicable for unlawful enemy combatants. Later several courts decided that went against the Constitution. Today anyone with a mobile device might be tracked despite how it might go against the Constitution.

The rights designated for all might continue to be gathered for a few, if people were prevented from questioning. The rights intended for all individuals might be increasingly extended to institutions if people don't follow the prescription given in the First Amendment.

The Patriot Act enhances surveillance procedure and diminishes privacy. One's spending habits, travel, reading material, bank accounts and communications are all now freely monitored, potentially in real time. Why is liberty removed for security? Where does elimination of liberty lead? Terrorist acts are deplorable and threatening, but perhaps a more real threat is the removal of liberty.

The Patriot Act acts as, but is not patriotism. The Patriot Act is jingoism and militarism, posing as patriotism. The real patriotic act is impossible to replace or supersede, the real patriot act is The First Amendment, the first right of individuals in the U.S.A.

All other Amendments are straightforward and pertain to particulars whereas the First Amendment is an amalgamation because it is the prescription of five stages of revolution in the form of an individual right. There are five distinct parts to the First Amendment which spell out five separate rights essential to maintain and expand liberty. These five procedures were formulated through observation of history, the story of the interplay between individuals and institutions.

Throughout history, the individual rights described in the First Amendment have been stomped out. Normally the stomping is done on a perceived "them" among an imagined "us" denoted by some institutionally conjured judgment. Exploitation has been institutionally and individually driven, but when individuals are run over on a large scale it practically always begins with the removal of their First Amendment rights, Five Freedoms. The First Amendment was enacted during the founding of the U.S.A. yet older cultures cherished these freedoms as well. The five rights of revolution in the First Amendment are question, communicate, speak out, stop and act.

Normally the First Amendment is only considered by way of the Five Freedoms, presented as the freedom of religion, speech, press, assembly and petition. This traditional presentation is wholly true, but softens the five rights of revolution in an institutionally safe interpretation, it waters them down. And perhaps this has served to trick people into thinking the First Amendment, the five rights of revolution, are applicable to institutions. In fact, The First Amendment was written specifically for individuals and not institutions. In fact, The First Amendment is about individual revolution against institutions, and cannot be meant for such machines, for institutions necessitate revolution in the first place. Institutions spawned a world where we have to say that we have these rights, otherwise it would just be inferred otherwise we would have maybe one or two laws and another that would be something similar to the Ninth Amendment.

The enumeration in the Constitution, of certain rights, shall not be construed to deny or disparage others retained by the people. ~Ninth Amendment

The Question - The Action

"In all fighting the direct method may be used for joining battle, but indirect methods will be needed in order to secure victory. Indirect tactics efficiently applied are inexhaustible as heaven and earth, unending as the flow of rivers and streams, like the sun and moon they end but to begin anew, like the four seasons they pass away to return once more.

There are not more than five musical notes, yet the combinations of these five give rise to more melodies than can ever be heard. There are not more than five primary colors; blue, yellow, red, white and black, yet in combination they produce more hues than can ever be seen. There are not more than five cardinal tastes; sour, acrid, salt, sweet, bitter, yet combinations yield more flavors than could ever be tasted.

In battle there are not more than two methods of attack; the direct and the indirect, yet these two in combination give rise to an endless series of maneuvers. The direct and the indirect lead on to each other in turn, it is like moving in a circle; you never come to an end. Who can exhaust the possibilities of their combination?"

~Sun Tzu

The First Amendment is first and foremost because it is the most powerful compilation of individual rights. Just as the pen is mightier than the sword, the First Amendment is mightier than the right to bear arms outlined in the Second Amendment. The First Amendment protects and also prescribes acts individuals can take to stand up to institutions.

The number five is symbolic for freedom, in part because we can free ourselves through using the five fingers of our hands. The five rights of revolution in the First Amendment act the same. The First Amendment reveals a step by step process to take peaceful and provocative action against institutional transgression. By practicing the five rights of revolution, as only an individual can, we practice the virtues necessary to develop individual and mass consciousness. The five rights, as applied to individuals, represent refined mankind. Affording them to institutions is like yielding to the idea of the divine right of kings.

"Congress shall make no law respecting an establishment of religion, or prohibiting the free exercise thereof; or abridging the freedom of speech, or of the press; or the right of the people peaceably to assemble, and to petition the Government for a redress of grievances." The First Amendment

Quo modo dium? What manner is god? Questions concerning the interpretation of god are the most rippling questions of all. Throughout history the interpretation of god and the reactions to divergent beliefs have caused some of the wildest events.

The first part of the First Amendment bestows the right to question the interpretation of god however one sees. Congress shall make no law prohibiting the free exercise of questions pertaining to the interpretation of God and all other subjects. People have the right to question the world and the universe, by way of any theory, by way of any interpretation of God. People have the right to question any subject up to and including the interpretation of God through any discipline. And people can question reality without utilizing interpretation of god at all. People have the right to question any subject, even established religious interpretations of god. No individual shall face repercussions for questioning the interpretation of God or any other question. Everyone has the right to question everything and exercise individual interpretations of everything, even God. When one is allowed to question interpretations of God then questioning all else is granted. No subject is above questioning and no institution, even those of God and government. In the same way when institutions representing God are allowed to be questioned questioning government institutions becomes easy. In the past pertinent questions pertaining to institutions of god and government were disallowed by the institutions.

There are five basic forms of asking questions. Who? What? Where? Why? When? How? When one is allowed to question god, one can question other dramatic subjects, which often go ignored, for people would rather ignore the status quo than question it, whether god or gas or nuclear experimentation.

To question and persevere in seeking answers is what separates mankind from antkind, curiosity and inventiveness sets man apart. The ability to question and develop with answers defines humanity. Asking questions and persistently seeking answers is a primordial gift that makes hands useful.

When questions go unasked, unanswered and are not promoted, there is potential of/for manipulation. It is the instinct of people, unburdened by fear to question all things great and small. When obvious and subtle questions go unasked, the cause is usually manipulation. When people are angered by questions, they are usually being manipulated or manipulating. Questioning relieves manipulation.

Oligarchic institutions prefer fewer questions be asked. And most institutions will eliminate questioning as much as people will tolerate. Great performances are enacted to eliminate questioning. These performances are done flagrantly and delicately, covertly and overtly. Institutions obviously and subtly portray themselves as having all the answers, especially those of god and government and imply they don't require questioning. The first part of the First Amendment provides unfettered right to the most powerful act of individuation, the defining right of revolution; questioning.

It is not that children are curious and adults lack curiosity; rather adults are manipulated into apathy. Calves are curious, cows are not. Adults acquire tolerations to speaking and accepting lies. Adults speak more lies more easily than children because they have developed tolerations to do so. People speak more lies, more frequently, more smoothly as they age and at the same time question actuality and the presentation of actuality less frequently. This is not a natural aging process, but manipulation.

Intelligent questions require no degree or title and neither should intelligent answers. Perhaps breath alone is the only requirement to question and hypothesize. People do not need to be accredited scholars to legitimately question conditions or situations, especially those of god and government. Some of the most profound and difficult questions are posed by children and apparent ignoramuses who know only the slightest of the subject in question. Some of the most brilliant and inventive people are not scholastic or official, but those who seek to answer questions.

To ask questions and to seek answers is the right and perhaps instinct of everyone and institutions attempt to remove this impetus and institute repercussions for stepping out of line. Questioning is the instinctual reaction of everyone over the age of two and a right fully utilized by few. Children instinctively ask "why?" and when they get an answer ask "why?" again endlessly and adults rarely do.

The same question can be seen as mundane curiosity or outright rebellion. What is in the water? Where does my food come from? What are genetically modified organisms? How does my tea get here? Does institution X intersect with institution Y? Why do they seek to control A through Z? Are political families simply involved in politics? What is the difference between an RPG and an IED? Why do we need the military industrial complex? Why is there promotion of nuclear experimentation? Why is there prohibition of marijuana cultivation? Why? Why? Why?

Question the questions and question the answers. Repeat. As long as you question everything, looking for truth, lies can't reside. Question individuals and question institutions that spend fortunes on public relations and propaganda creating an image, logo and message. Question those who claim they cannot be wrong and those who claim to have all the answers.

Question those who would openly enact wrong for something they claim is greater than right. Don't believe every fact, statistic, statement or interpretation of fact presented, especially those of officials, but look into it for yourself. Why do they require so many facts and stats? Why? Why? Why? Officials have more reasons to present partial truths than revolutionaries. Question institutions that spend fortunes to encourage people to do something, buy something or believe something.

Lacking questions allows the netherworld oligarchy. The lack of questioning and the squashing of questions permitted and enabled the invasion of Iraq for instance. The U.S.A. House of Representatives were presented with flawed information and investigations were left undone, questions were unasked. There are countless hearts and minds who wish they questioned more, or at all.

The documents used to install the war were lies by omission if not bold faced lies and yet were written by officials, trusted institutional branches of the U.S.A.

government tree. If reputable institutions with resourced information can be wrong or lie, any institution can be wrong or lie. Also, dichotomously, any unofficial individual may be correct, not automatically, but equally likely. Lord Acton's rule states they that power corrupts and absolute power corrupts absolutely requiring the likes of pope and king be questioned more so than individuals because they have so much to gain and lose. You can't trust powerful institutions ever and you can trust average individuals sometimes.

Ignorance is strength to institutions. Perhaps the majority of people are not being sickened from a polluted environment profiting a select minority. Perhaps manufacturing weapons is meant to deter their use. Perhaps building prisons is meant to scare away would-be criminals. Perhaps marijuana is illegal to protect individuals and society. Perhaps nuclear experimentation will deform us into immortals. Perhaps global slavery doesn't exist. Perhaps institutions of god, government and goods have not formed an oligarchical collective over individuals. Of course it would take questioning to know. Don't believe institutions just because. Question, or carry on. Question, or keep listening to institutions as they guide you on the road more traveled. Institutions are glad to tell you what is happening, where you should go, what you should buy and how you should think so you have to question information from those who have power and influence.

Question all statements, but follow Lord Acton's rule and question powerful institutions more. Look into the presentation and coordination of information and action. Look into information provided by established institutions. Often what is stated is different from what is meant, and sometimes what is meant is different than what is interpreted. And sometimes people lie. And those with institutional powers lie more frequently than anyone. No matter what information is presented, complete or partial, rhetorical or factual, theoretical or practical, all information requires questioning in order to realize if it is reality or fiction.

Mathematical statistics and calculations are capable of being obviously and subtly distorted. Statistical interpretation of situations within states was first taken into account by empires in the 1600s. Goddfried Achenwall first termed the phrase statistic, meaning science of the state. Statistics was also called "political arithmetic" in its beginnings. It is not considered to be mathematics, but uses math. Goddfried received financial support from King George III. The Same King George III who inspired revolution, the same royal oligarchical leader the colonists fought the Revolutionary War against.

The system of checks and balances, the very basis of the framework of U.S.A. government, exists to enable questions and keep in check the oligarchy. It is the underlying concept, the very essence behind the design of the U.S.A. To question is the most fundamental special right that people have. To question and check information, balances. The first nuclear meltdown in the U.S.A. occurred in California. And it wasn't until the meltdown at Three Mile Island that people questioned and found out about the meltdowns at the experimental Santa Susana site in Simi Valley. The meltdown were apparently much smaller than the Three Mile Island reactor, but released over two hundred times the radiation.

In ancient times all teaching was done orally and all stories were simple dialogues in art because it's a great way to impart information. The ancient Hindus and Greeks practically always related their stories as dialogues. Communication is not unique among humans alone, but the nuances and abstracts that humans are capable of communicating, differentiates us from the rest of the animal world. In order to communicate openly, toward truth, it is important to accept information and openly relay information. Be accepting, but do not just accept anything anyone tells you without questioning it. Be skeptical of answers, but also be skeptical of questions and skeptical of skepticism. Do not refuse information as institutions often do. Acknowledge information from various sources. Individuals have the right to accept and question information from all sources and communicate concerns with any of it. Individuals can decry falsehood as well. Institutions will go so far as to refuse to accept the existence of whole national institutions and individuals therein. Perhaps the greatest example of refusal to accept information is the United States' refusal to recognize the nation of Israel has nuclear weapons.

Biased and partial information is abundant, yet this is not reason to castoff information before contemplation and communication; this is reason to acquire more information from more sources. It is as equally important to question confirmed information as it is to generally ignore information from confirmed liars. Ignorance is excusable; acceptance of lies is inexcusable.

The ability to freely share and consider information is a rarity. Individuals are capable of open communication, yet this ability is not always engaged. Institutions and the institutionalized normally restrict and limit the information they consider and deliver.

Institutions do not accept all answers, even if the truth is therein. All institutions, especially states, do not accept information from certain sources if they do not meet the particular institutional qualifications to be heard, seen and spoken of. Those that do not meet requirements are ignored. Institutions do not recognize new information unless it is from a source deemed acceptable and then they eat whatever is fed to them without asking what's in it.

On top of disregarding certain information, many institutions also don't consider the totality of otherwise widely accepted information. They negate some information, and then don't properly consider information that they have accepted. Institutions are guilty of another contravention of communication, withholding information that they have accepted from others. Institutions are not capable of open communication. They always distort or withhold information predominantly closing parameters.

The first part of the First Amendment applied institutionally allows them to set their agenda upon society using money as their voice. Corporate government collectivism has been promoted and expanded, but now with the institutions united decision of the Supreme Court 'corporations are people too my friend.' Institutions have been bestowed with the rights of individuals.

To question all information, to consider and discuss all potential answers with others is not only a right, it's human nature. Communication is a primal instinctual urge that has enabled man to fly and have light at night. To question, to consider and reveal information openly removes a cornerstone from the pyramid system of the netherworld oligarchy.

The fundamental structure of a pyramidal oligarchy is compartmentalized architecture and information. Compartmentalization is liberated by open exchange. Tell everyone known information and accept the information of others, even if –no- especially if they are informing you of things you do not want to hear. Institutions withhold and omit information to essentially divide and conquer, or at least divide and profit. And they prefer that others do the same.

"(Congress shall make no law respecting) abridging the freedom of speech,"

Let everyone know who is capable of understanding because ideas are bettered through communication. Most media sources, it seems, function to distribute limited interpretations of reality rather than simple investigative reports of reality. Institutions prefer swift stories of little merit because they support the status quo. Institutions communicate their side of the story well, or the side of the story they want you to hear, but do not accept all information openly or openly communicate. Questioning and communicating provides impetus and structure for peaceful revolution.

It is our nature to share information. No matter how alienated people are, they cannot be fooled when in possession of information and become less alienated with information. The same way domesticated dogs and Capuchin monkeys tend to share food, people tend to share information as well as resources. People desire open communication and when unburdened of limited resources and limited information we share. The American Indians made markings to show future hunters where the game congregated.

Imagine a General Electric media outlet, be it NBC, Disney or Time doing a story on GE's pollution of the Hudson River, or Housatonic River, or Saratoga County, Spokane County, Henderson County or Puerto Rico or their flawed nuclear reactor designs -flawed according to scientists formerly employed by GE- which went into meltdown, melt-throughs in Fukushima after an earthquake in the most seismically active region of the planet. Their story would probably be limited in scope and likely would never be presented at all in entirety or properly. Now imagine institutions with ties to other institutions creating other polluted situations and covering them up. Of course institutions are going to leave these situations unmentioned. Such oligarchical institutionalization limits information and produces lies.

The energy institutions of the world are arguably some of the most powerful and, in accordance with Lord Acton's rule, some of the most corrupt. When the Chernobyl nuclear experimentation disaster occurred there were many lies, however one lie demonstrates the institutional tendency to lie so as not to lead to questioning and communication. The French nuclear agency lied about Chernobyl so as to eliminate questions about their own nuclear experiments. The French authorities stated that there was no way any radioactive material from the Chernobyl disaster made it into France because there happens to be a vortex due to the English Channel and the Alps, which blows any such material away from France. Years later, spikes in thyroid cancer from radioactive iodine proved this to be false. Today France the most nuclear nation, about 75% of the power in France comes from nuclear experiments.

Institutional interconnectedness results in oligarchical collectivism. That's why church and state institutions remain separate in the United States. And that is why corporate and state institutions should be separate. Perhaps the bias and lack of complete information is purposeful. Perhaps GE and other corporations would like history to present GE as an ignorant polluter of the era of world war and not a profiteer. GE would like people to believe they are innocent of wrongdoing, and not question how they have fought to avoid cleanup of and compensation for the messes leftover from their profits. Progression and revolution are halted when communication is limited.

If there were only one source of information, or only a few, as presumably GE would like it, then there would be less variation of ideas, less instigation of questions and very little progression and revolution. The fewer sources of information, the less likely consequences and conditions will be properly questioned and considered. The larger the institution presenting information, the more likely their information is going to be distorted in some way by some confluence at their roots.

Open exchange of information is the best way to impart liberty. Allowing people to speak openly without repercussion is part of liberty. If they are wrong, tell them, if they are exploiting, by all means retort and redress the, but let them speak and expose themselves for how wrong they are, and then maybe more people will question them next time. The ability to communicate openly and without threat is a founding principle of the U.S.A. The freedoms to question and communicate are the first rights to revolution and the first rights to be eliminated by despots.

Enacting and practicing open communication is indicative of quality human behavior. If they are wrong, tell them, tell everyone, but let them communicate without threat. Communication leads to betterment of ideas and if communication leads to ideas better than your own be grateful. But be wary when informing others of valid and disagreeable information. Some people will attack the messenger instead of acknowledging and disputing their information. If information is sensitive in one way or another, they will attack syntax, accent or neck, and always disregard.

In the netherworld oligarchy ignorance may get you sick or killed. To simply enjoy the beauty of one's surroundings was once completely satisfying. Today, one has to take care to be sure that the environment is not dangerous, that the water is safe to drink or swim in or fish from.

What good is the right to question if no one questions? If no one seeks answers or if everyone merely questions irrelevant subject matter than the First Amendment's revolutionary potential is not being used. If people only communicate about irrelevant subject matter or worse only communicate with people who believe the same things than progression and revolution will not be activated. Withholding information is dear to institutions, while equal dispersal of information is dear to individuals, or should be.

The best thing to do with information is to share it amongst the majority. Once that information is available, new information is uncovered and developed. Truth can always be improved upon with more truth. The shaking caused by paradigms is slighted and smoothed when open dispersal of information is practiced.

Tell everyone, even if they feel they are being told off. Don't withhold relevant information so as not to rattle sensitivity. Communicate no matter the resulting disturbance. Be accepting to everyone, but question everyone, not as insult, but as courtesy. Communication dismantles bad ideas, betters good ideas and finds the difference between the two. If, by being divided we are conquered, then by being united we are unconquerable. To be united, information and resources must be openly available to all. To be united people need an understanding of others, to understand others people need to communicate. Only by functioning in alternative terms can one create alternatives to the netherworld oligarchy. To truly defy the pyramid system, operate in circular capacity instead of holding a pyramidal perspective. Be peaceful and treat others as equals in the circle.

"You have noticed that everything an Indian does is in a circle and that is because the power of the world always works in circles, and everything tries to be round...the sky is round, and I have heard that the earth is round like a ball, and so are all the stars. The wind, in its greatest power, whirls. Birds make their nest in circles, for theirs is the same religion as ours....even the seasons form a great circle in their changing, and always come back again to where they were. The life of a man is a circle from childhood to childhood, and so it is in everything where power moves." ~Black Elk

Be accepting of everyone and tell everyone everything, then the institutionalized viewpoint that only privileged should be in the know is defeated. By sharing information one distributes power and equality. Julian Asange shared information about institutional manipulations. The intercepted institutional communications were about manipulations of the netherworld oligarchy. A series of diplomatic orders insisted that there should be harsh consequences for those European nations who refused genetically modified organisms. What do ambassadors care about force feeding corporculture GMO to Europe?

By openly sharing and accepting information pyramidal slant is flattened. The oligarchical pyramid system is havoc upon fairness; exploitation. Accepting others and openly providing information unites and eliminates problems derived from labeling people based on their location, heritage, appearance, or institutional alignment.

Information is power. When whole and true information is openly exchanged, a whole and true point of view is established. When information is shared, everyone is uplifted. When the presentation of information is intentionally limited, it is in order to control perception. Open communication alone can often lead to revolution.

Diplomacy is communication between national institutions. They either accept information from other institutions or deny and decry information presented from unallied institutions. Institutions have steeply slanted biases concerning what information they accept and distribute. Those who do not walk and talk the mutual institutional line are ignored by institutions. Be an individual. Accept and relay truthful information and decry the lies no matter the sources.

Those who believe differently are not necessarily unworthy of computing information. Their different opinion is from different information. If you want people to listen to you, listen to them and question everyone, especially yourself. Remind those of differing opinions that open dialogue is mutually empowering and will only lead to a better understanding for all. Open exchange of information leads to more coherent observations, inventions and revolution. Dialectic exchange leads to development of better tools.

Communication is required to determine the best symbol to build or destroy so as to gather enough individual focus for a revolutionary turn. Only through communication can circular alternatives to the pyramidal netherworld oligarchy be shared. Revolutionaries are glad to stop the status quo without plan for new direction, assuming that on stopping the terrain can be better surveyed and new course taken. Unfortunately most people are not revolutionary. Most people would rather stay with the plan even if it means doom. And so a symbol must be destroyed or constructed to snap people out of their trance.

The symbol should inspire questioning and dialectical discussion. If the symbolic model works and instigates discussion on the status quo many dependent on the system will try to degrade the symbolism as hollow. When an institution is confronted they will rally against the opposition and imply ignorance leaning on official and quantifiable this and that. However sometimes things that are important are mostly unquantifiable.

There is an old indigenous tale of a tribe who considered birds a delicacy. They liked eating the birds so much that they ultimately ate them all. And then the tribe began to sadden. Only then did they realize that the food was good but the birdsong was much more important to their happiness. For revolutionaries saving the birdsong is enough. For the institutionalized following the behaviors dictated by the majority is sensible and taking new course requires sway to their comfort.

There is another old fable with a life lesson using a bird as the comparative tool. A small, little bird ended up stuck on a boat in the middle of the ocean. The ship encounters a great storm and the little bird, with nowhere to go, finds a perch and rides the storm out. The bird has no tears and no fears. The bird remains proud through the most volatile of storms, no matter the outcome. Every bird, great and small, colorful or drab, is proud until death, no matter what. Every animal behaves this way –proudly, every animal except man. Revolutionaries behave proudly in storms as opposed to most of modern man, behaving not proudly, but docilely.

Those who cry on encountering a storm or any set of waves and change, even change focused on elimination of evil are easily rattled because being docile leads to desire for routine, even if the routine is negative and the change is positive. Instead of destroying the environment through onetime extraction build the environment through sustainable and productive permaculture. Instead of fencing in the garden open it up.

Instead of creating some genetically modified organism dependent on toxins, use what is naturally reliable, productive and sustainable. Hemp is the loveliest and productive plant there is. It is the plant they all wish they could genetically modify and makes all genetic modification a waste of money and an obvious franchise operation to sell toxins and postmodernism. Hemp can feed the world and supply us with the raw materials to make paper, clothing, housing and oil. Hemp grows without pesticides. Hemp can boost the economy and help eliminate the toxin based "conventional" corporate monoculture. Hemp based biofuel could eliminate the need for global petrol mining and burning.

Solar energy could replace nuclear power plants. Wind, wave and ocean current technology could transform the netherworld oligarchy. The amount of money your average nuclear plant costs plus the global environmental ramifications of the triple meltthrough in Fukushima and the Chernobyl meltdown plus the unknown and relatively localized releases of radioactive particulate are incalculably costly compared to solar power installations whether in series, utilizing the electric grid already in place or in more concentrated solar panel fields using different technology. Solar power implementation could incontrovertibly replace nuclear power generation. Using "current-mills", underwater turbines to tap ocean current steadily whirling with tremendous force could also replace nuclear experimentation both fiscally and physically.

Implementation of agriculturally sourced fuels would produce steady and immediate job opportunity. Initiation of solar power generation would also as well as maintenance job opportunity in the future. The solution would be an economic boon and creative inspiration. It would enliven and enrich us all instead continual submission to franchise corporate mob rule with apparently no direction, but down further into the netherworld oligarchy pit. We have the technology. The problem is the oligarchy.

"(Congress shall make no law respecting the establishment) of the press,"

Allowing the free exchange of information and unbiased communication without repercussion is a higher function of collectives. Investigation, possession and release of information exemplifies higher intellect and spirituality. Those who readily speak are among the bravest individuals. No other animal can present explanations, exclamations and proclamations as complex as man. Only people have the ability speak out on behalf of themselves and others and only brave people do so. Alternatively only people can hide information making the press so necessary.

They came first for the Communists, and I didn't speak up because I wasn't a Communist.

Then they came for the Jews, and I didn't speak up because I wasn't a Jew.

Then they came for the trade unionists, and I didn't speak up because I wasn't a trade unionist.

Then they came for the Catholics, and I didn't speak up because I was a Protestant.

Then they came for me, and by that time no one was left to speak up.

Martin Niemoller, Theologian

The reason for the freedom of the press is to inform people of transgressions. Individuals and institutions try to hide all sorts of trespasses and if it were not for the press investigating, questioning, provoking, recording, quoting and providing historical relevance all sorts of wrong might be slid down the memory hole.

The press speaks out to peers and strangers alike. The press speaks up for everybody as the savior of Martin Niemoller apathy everywhere. The press is skeptical and suspicious, always. The press ought to befriend no one and certainly should not attend parties with politicians.

When you are otherwise a stranger, people only recognize you for what you express. Often they might think you represent an agenda of sorts. Perhaps one's opinions are based out of an institutionalization of sorts. Realization of the institutionalization of oneself and others is more likely after speaking out. American exceptionalism impels us to speak out. Many cultures make it so people only do so when there is nothing left to lose, for the consequences are so severe they might lose everything. The Press in the U.S.A. is known as the fourth branch of government, for the free information distribution checks and balances as much as or more than the three branches of government. The free press keeps transparency, but we are losing that tendency and tolerating the overall inclination shade transparency and put the institution first.

Speaking out develops opinions, for speaking out cries for response and discourse. Before speaking out be prepared for debate and detraction. You will find there are many interpretations to what you say and many counterpoints that may not have been considered when you reach a large audience. The process of respectful open debate should be encouraged and the presentation of information, no matter how consequential or trifle, should never be met with consequences –in a free society with First Amendment rights. Yet reporters are routinely threatened, beaten and killed by all sorts, but always for the same reason; revealing information.

There are many means to speak out. One's voice is the primary format. In the late 1700s, when the First Amendment was drafted, the printing press was the pinnacle technology. In the information age one's voice is amplified and enabled by the exponentially technological expanding ability to communicate.

Individuals can speak out often in equally powerful concepts as institutions only with less audience. Institutions simply have higher podium to speak from.

Individuals don't have to say much, but may speak out simply through spending habits and utilization of purchasing power.

"It does not require many words to speak the truth." ~Chief Joseph

"In an age of universal deceit, telling the truth becomes a revolutionary act." ~George Orwell

The institutions united, called the Citizen's United Supreme Court decision enabled any entity to donate unlimited funds to political campaigns –as a manner through which to speak out. Any corporation usually headed by one or a few individuals can now push an agenda and effectively fund the media campaign of any politician. It effectively reinvigorates the divine right of kings only it the divine right institutions. Speaking out informs large groups of people, like the intended design of political action committees. Informing large groups of people of the entire truth, instead of omitted portions, disrupts the pyramid system of the netherworld oligarchy with a circle. Speaking out is standing up and defying the majority, like the freed prisoner, like the rebellious slave and like the uberman.

Speaking out communicates, sometimes without need for word or image. Speaking out requires an understanding of actuality and a brave heart to face informed as well as ignorant opposition. Speaking out may take place among an audience that is too large to communicate with or by means that does not enable communication. Speaking out communicates, however it is a statement often without forum for debate or rebuttal. To speak out, one has to stand up and inform others, without intention of exchanging direct communication, but rather to stimulate overall communication.

(Congress shall make no law respecting)...the right of the people peaceably to assemble,

Anyone can speak out by themselves, including via destruction or construction of symbols, but when people come together to speak out on their own instead of through some institutional supported pursuit it is more meaningful. When fifty thousand people show up for a sporting event it is nothing, if fifty thousand people protest war or prison it is highly noteworthy. And the netherworld oligarchical authorities despise individuals coming together to question or communicate or worse speak out. We can see that dominant institutions seek to quell individuals coming together in protest the same way as in the violently repressed Russian Revolution as well as protests of police violence in Anaheim, 2012. Institutions are given podiums to speak out to random people and the podiums are protected by the martial authority of the oligarchy. Individuals need to grab moments to speak out when they can, find illustrious and illustrative symbols to build or destroy and come together. Most individuals normally have less access to the audience than institutions have by way of the Institutions United decision which cemented the idea that money equates voice. More importantly individuals have no protection from the aggressive reactions of authorities or other supporters of the status quo. Individuals without podiums need to join together when speaking out, when construction and destruction symbols.

Institutions respect and answer to individuals, but only when the numbers are adequate, either the numbers speaking or listening. If five individuals speak out, they probably will be ignored or vacated by authorities. If there are five hundred, they will probably get beat up or broken up and locked down by authorities, perhaps protests numbering five thousand would be similarly violated. But if there is a protest of fifty thousand or five hundred thousand, the authorities will allow the protest to take place. In the same way if one person represents many thousands they are more likely to be appeased. Attempts to neutralize the effectiveness of protests may take place no matter, but even the martial oligarchical collectivist bashers have to address large and persistent numbers. When enough individuals unify, they quantify and qualify institutional requirements of recognition.

"One finger cannot lift a pebble." ~Hopi proverb

The institutionalized authorities are designed to hold back and incite violence. Individual protests are designed to instigate insight, in part by construction and destruction symbols. If institutionalized arms of authority are given legal reason, legal opportunity or orders to enforce violently, they will. And sometimes they will simply give a warning over a loud speaker, so they are then legally allowed to change people's lives with nonlethal weapons as the Bay Area police officers did when they broke up the Occupy Oakland demonstrations and shot Scott Olsen in the head with a nonlethal device.

Individuals have to call attention to violence to defeat it. We have to stand up to it and occasionally the institutions are so repugnantly ruthless we take a beating the process. Opportunity for institutions to do so can arise from simply lacking numbers or just crossing whatever arbitrary line is drawn by the authorizing institutions. Institutional authorities want to stop protests, while protesters want to raise awareness of and stop wrongdoing, normally wrongdoing conducted by institutions in control of the authorities.

Numbers matter to institutions. Numbers measure people and money and numbers. Institutions have no heart, but the machines can count. A group of people who speak out on an issue as a cohesive unit, otherwise nonaligned, sharing only a statement on the situation, can have real sway and real say concerning the actions of institutions. By speaking as one, many can change and spur peaceful revolution, but it only takes one to spur the many. The more are involved in a statement, the more direct the message should be and the more difficult it gets to keep things simple, but there are some things we all can agree on, the five interconnected netherworld instigators. Focus on one institution at a time. Movement requires focus.

Oligarchical institutions have latched onto the rights of individuals and used them to promote their own interests, while many individuals do not use the rights prescribed to them to protect their interests. You have more rights than any institution. They would like you to believe otherwise, they want you to think they have more power, but they do not have heart. Individuals are alive, institutions are not. Institutions are tools. The status quo of the netherworld oligarchy is too elaborate to be controlled with force alone, but nothing is too massive to be controlled by information and idea. The same goes for confrontation of the massive status quo, it cannot be confronted with force, but with open information.

"It is true you may fool all of the people some of the time: you can even fool some of the people all of the time: but you can't fool all of the people all of the time." ~Abraham Lincoln

But they can try. And if they can fool enough people sometimes, the fools fool more people just by being foolish. When the unfooled speak out, they not only succeed in exerting possible influence over the fooled, they also show people who aren't fooled that there are others with them. The freedom of the press is the freedom to express and progress truth and eliminate potential foolishness. Relaying information has to be done in order to uplift people, gathering together is the irrefutable statement.

Whether in telling the Socratic Allegory of the Cave and the prisoner-captor dynamic or it is revealing that what corporations call family farms are comparable to generational slavery relaying and revealing information is grand, eliminating it and distorting it is usually done at the request of institutions. Mark Twain popularized the sentiment that there are three types of lies; lies, damned lies, and statistics. However there are actually four types of lies institutions use to control the situation. To put it simply lies arrive in the addition of information, the subtraction of information, the multiplication of extraneous information and the division of relevant information.

The builders and destroyers of symbols have to understand lies so as to expose them. You got to do the math. There are many ways to construct and destroy symbols, sometimes all that is required is a little arithmetic and action. Doing the math and presenting the solution can change things from the outside or inside.

The best way to effect change on mass consciousness is to change your individual consciousness first. Change things by changing oneself. Join something or create something to join. Speak out from the inside as an individual concerned for individuals. Sometimes it is effective to throw over the table, like Jesus did, other times it is more efficient to sit at the table and calmly explain. If circumstances are fair and pleasant then leave well enough alone. However in the netherworld oligarchy, the rarity of gold is eclipsed by the rarity of conditions that would not benefit from change.

Explain and exclaim the interconnectedness and institutional transgressions. The U.S.A. is based on free speech, everyone deserves forum, whether in official halls or the hills or anywhere in between we have the same rights no matter the setting. Your voice is your strength.

We should demand there be hard copies of our votes. Just the possibility that electronic voting machines could be tampered with should convince people of every county and country to question their exactness and trustworthiness. Speak up! Speak up for yourself and speak up for others or stay in line and shut up. Maybe people weren't meant to fly, but we were certainly meant to speak out.

"All our lauded technological progress - our very civilization - is like an axe in the hands of a pathological criminal."
Albert Einstein

Nuclear waste has nowhere go and few speak of this endless peril. In 2013 the U.S.A. allowed increased amounts of radiation in consumer products.

Besides the usual release of radiation from weapons tests, processing, power generation, falling satellites, sinking submarines, underwater dumping of radioactive material and war, more industries increasingly use radioactive materials for more diverse applications. Even food is irradiated by radioactive rays, euphemistically labeled cold pasteurization.

"I am not only a pacifist but a militant pacifist. I am willing to fight for peace. Nothing will end war unless people themselves refuse to go to war. "
Albert Einstein

Nuclear experimentation devices were exploded in all strata of Earth Mother just to investigate their destructive power. The waste is buried in deep caverns in attempts to be rid of it. Some waste has been launched into outer space. All life on the planet was risked in the process of an acceleration technique called the slingshot when one and perhaps more than one satellite from the U.S.S.R loaded with waste was launched around the moon to return to Earth to be effectively slung into space through interaction with Earth's gravity. If the calculations were off, all of us might have experienced plutonium rain. Several satellites with nuclear power generators were launched into orbit, doomed to return and rain down radiation. The exact number of how many nuclear reactor powered satellites fell from space is unknown. Many submarine reactors are now cast away under the oceans too.

Waste is buried and shot into space, but there is already too much rotting in fuel pools at power generation experiments with nowhere to go for the next couple of million years. Nuclear power is not clean energy, it is institutionalized and monopolized energy fit only for the netherworld oligarchy to benefit the 00000000.1%.

Fuck nuclear power generation and fuck nuclear experimentation in total. Sometimes you have to stand up say something wild to get people's attention in a war economy where the likes of Karl Rove use war for political ends. Nuclear experimentation is a tool for the military industrial complex which is a global multifaceted arrangement of institutions designed to control and kill people. All nations relying on nuclear experimentation are doomed to fail. Soon after the Chernobyl event, the USSR collapsed. Now the world community is trying to prevent more catastrophic releases by building another structure to contain it. Japan is crippled, soon to be a nation of sick and dying bewildered because of the ever increasing radiation release from the multiple meltthroughs and reactor/fuel pool issues at Fukushima. But even the Japanese, stuck effectively drinking uranium tea won't eat GMO from the U.S.A. The Monsanto unapproved GMO rogue wheat found growing in Oregon inspired the Japan and other nations to restrict U.S.A. wheat imports in 2013.

Fuck the military industrial complex for installing nuclear power generation experimentation on the most seismically active places in the world, a whole island of volcanic, geothermal, wind, wave and ocean current energy potential. Fuck the EPA for turning off access to its formerly public radiation monitors A.F. (After Fukushima) and whoever told them to do so. Look at how it took two years for the mainstream media to admit that there was an environmental catastrophe, impacting the living and the unborn. Look how it took TEPCO over two years to get the math correct. And look how government and media institutions followed TEPCO's math without their own. The supposed alternative media was years ahead in breaking news from Fukushima.

Peace on Earth and fuck war. Sometimes you have to stop right where you are and stand up for something. Let them insult you for it, but talk with them calmly after you get their attention with an expletive. Or let them call you out for your vulgar use of language and then inform then that their own vulgarity, their despicable actions are much worse than any use of language. Let it set a course for the debate on which is more drastic and which requires more attention, the momentary use of foul language or the unyielding ever present global state of war which is right now killing the unborn in the name of doomed national institutions. Global war makes it so you have to use some wild language to obtain the attention of the dumbfounded. Imagine the insults that were thrown at the people who first said that some in the Catholic Church had been abusing children for decades, and others covered it up, worldwide. Imagine suggesting the world is a globe, when it suits the authorities that it is a cube.

The world is a pyramid. We live in the pyramidal netherworld oligarchy to the Nth degree. The exact calculations of its dimensions and the exact interlocking of the institutions will not be revealed on the evening news. In fact the evening news primarily reports on the trite fuck you statements of the day rather than investigating what institution is fucking you. The streets know first, because people know first. Just as the streets knew about the perverted Catholic priests way before the major media covered it and just as the alternative media covered the effects of radiation on the unborn before the major media. The streets know first and the major media either yields to the voice of the streets or presents information to counter it.

What is most important in life? If there is clean air and water, if there is adequate food and resources, all else is granted. If there are not such simple requirements, questions are necessary. It is possible to stop eating temporarily; no panic should ensue if one misses a meal especially in doing something as noble as gathering with others to protest wrongdoing. Gandhi occasionally fasted for his health as well a form of protest. The longest fast in protest is attributed to Terence Macswiney, 74 days to death. Terrence was an Irish writer and politician arrested by the British Government on charges of sedition in 1920. He immediately began a hunger strike protesting his internment and trial before a military court.

People routinely fast for various reasons. Other people routinely go without adequate nutrition. A fast is a temporary pause, malnutrition and hunger is constant desperation. People can survive for weeks without food, but only a few days without clean water and only a few moments without clean oxygen. Recent studies conclude that simply eating less food is healthy, but we all need healthy food, clean air and water.

Institutions of the netherworld oligarchy possess power in action. Individuals possess power in inaction. The power of the individual rests in the ability to diffuse institutions, in the ability to do nothing and disobey. And when individuals take inaction institutions fall by the wayside, the more useless they are the faster they fall off. When institutions stop they are disempowered, when individuals stop they are empowered.

Individuals have power that institutions do not. No matter how much money and property institutions amass individuals possess consciousness. A conscious individual with clear focus is more powerful than any institution. Institutions fear such individuals. Such individuals are capable of self-rule, no longer requiring institutions to control every step. Gandhi called it swaraj, meaning self-rule or home rule. The idea is to allow local individuals to set their own course, for local communities to be independent from some distant and centralized authority.

Stop to protest. Stop to observe the elements, to meditate, or investigate. Stop to peaceably assemble. And stop to see what the authorities do to people who stop together. Stop to see who is pulling the strings and contemplate the rigidity of the netherworld oligarchy. Wrongdoing occurs during extremes. Stop and relax. Slow down. Be balanced. You, acting in unison with others, can change the world by simply reducing your consumption and specifically ceasing support of offending institutions. You, acting in unison with others, can change institutions nonviolently. Cease institutional support for a day, a week, stop one thing for a year and rally others to do so. Stop, for stopping is the best way to start something new.

If corporations think of you as a consumer, power rests in your spending habits. Stop spending, stop fueling, stop showing up or stop somewhere and stay there to make a statement. Institutional machines are fireproof, bulletproof and don't leave anything off the table, but they need constant attention and maintenance. If enough people stop greasing the machine the machine stops. And so institutions do all they can to stop movements from catalyzing and causing change.

The best things in life are free, and that which is priceless you can't buy. Family, friends, peers and potential new friends are priceless. Time, fresh air and fresh water are priceless. Institutions and machines are lifeless. Absolutely each and every one of them has a price. All lifeless institutions all together are not worth the priceless things they destroy.

To stop specific actions completely is not absurd when continuing manifests such ridiculous hazards to life now and in the future. Stopping is a difficult notion to accept because it is not among the building blocks of the status quo, not within the pyramid system, but it is easy to do. Everyone is trained to continue wrong, despite the wrong, no matter the resulting wrong. We have to shift that institutionalized mentality to an indigenous one. Stopping wrong is easy and effective with potential for extraordinary, even lucrative results for stopping allows starting.

Ceasing support of institutions in protest might be decried as un-American (or some other institutional rhetoric) in a culture of separation, in fact it is righteous and un-institutional, in fact it is in line with and prescribed by the First Amendment. In fact it goes against training and institutionalization. Institutions insist on continuation regardless of negative outcome. Who will argue stopping what is wrong despite the consequences? Who will argue discontinuing riding the shiny status quo with the rotting underbelly? Those who feed off it, that's who.

This netherworld oligarchy contains conflicts, consequences, conditions and confines negative to existence and yet it benefits a finite few just enough to somehow enable it. And the whole world has been conned and fleeced of clean air and water for the profit of a few. Cooperation with our natural surroundings, sustainability has yielded to mechanization and institutionalization.

Coexistence between people, places and things is possible, but less likely the more rigid the surrounding institutions. No matter the powers authorities may display, people are always able to stand up to their authority. There is no institution that people cannot dismantle by standing together righteously and reasonably. There is no institution that can force people to continue if they are committed to stopping. Stopping is the most powerful act and alternatively there is nothing institutions won't do to prevent individuals from doing so.

In June 1989, there were protests throughout all of China. The protests were countrywide, but were centered in Tiananmen Square, Beijing, one of the largest public spaces in the world. People gathered to peacefully protest and soldiers aggressively converged on the students and citizens. Fighting amongst the armed soldiers and civilians ensued. The timeless archetypal story of unarmed countrymen, locals, oppressed people gathering together only to be confronted by armed soldiers began again. The scene might have been St. Petersburg in 1905 or any other stately repressive reaction to protests.

Possibly thousands were killed in Beijing, definitely hundreds. Many more were injured, the exact numbers are unknown. What is known is that the protest and unrest was a bloodbath. People were confronted with the armed forces. People expressed themselves by communicating, speaking up and most threatening to the institutions, stopping their roles and gathering together. They were confronted and soldiers shot civilians.

Tanks eventually arrived on the scene to secure the area. On the morning of June 5, 1989 a column of tanks began a procession around Tiananmen Square. One lone individual stepped in front of the lead tank and stopped. He just stood there, preventing the parade of tanks and the show of force. He stopped in the middle of the street while apparently carrying groceries and a book bag. The column of tanks all stopped and some turned off their engines. He climbed onto the tank and yelled at the driver. Eventually, he was taken away by people who are theorized to be police. The unknown rebel was never seen or heard from again.

Take a stand, stop. Stop, if only for a few minutes like tank-man or those at the Boston Tea Party, Thoreau, Gandhi, Martin Luther King Jr. and so many countless others. Keep in mind that tanks are likely to run you over if you step in front of them, and institutional agents might sweep you away, but there are other ways individuals can diminish and stop the power of machinery, even tanks. The Tiananmen Square protests were quelled with violence.

The most powerful act is to stop, defy and disobey. Simply ceasing wrongdoing is the best way to implement change. Through questioning and communicating one can understand actuality, through speaking out one can call attention to situations and through stopping one can have an impact. If enough wrongdoing is stopped, bettered situations can be conceptualized and actualized. Most institutions and institutionalized don't know how to operate outside of the status quo. Only individuals can invent and implement anew and often only when the old is ceased.

Solar energy could free the world from permanent reliance on oligarchical energy. Solar power is not expensive, it is free. Combined with renewable wind power, geothermal power and hydroelectricity, there would be no concern for energy. There are numerous sources of natural and perpetual energy, it is here, occurring now. It is only a matter of tapping into it and better utilizing what is already available. Hemp could also be grown as a complete alternative to petrol fuels. Wind, wave and solar energy are constant and clean sources of energy. Ocean currents could be harnessed with underwater turbines. There are many sources of energy besides the guts of Earth Mother.

There are many forms of energy that are more sensible for life than mineral sources. There are many sources of energy available that would provide equal power to people with fewer complications. However, there are not many forms of energy that would provide equal power to oligarchical institutions with as many compliments.

Sometimes wrong ideas prevent us from seeing the right way, as if smog settled onto a cityscape. We could have energy that would be relatively free of negative environmental costs. The transformation could cost billions, but what is the cost of fueling the netherworld oligarchy? Free and renewable energy is a great idea for individuals, but not for institutions. Free energy is not conducive to elite control, free energy sheds institutional dependence.

What does oil cost? What does oil earn?

What does war cost? What does war earn?

Free energy would remove a cornerstone in the pyramid system. Free energy provides independence and institutions would lose power and relevance. Humanity could have had limitless, free energy a long time ago, but institutions prefer to maintain the status quo. Why provide something for free when they can get paid for it?

Perhaps global warming is just a passing phase, instigated by the sun, but the atmospheric damage humanity is causing, the toxicity of the culture of separation is absolutely verifiable and can be diluted no more. The high and mighty seas can no longer disperse man's poisonous wake, the wide skies and winds can no longer blow it away.

Individuals experience, institutions do not. They do not drink or breathe or feel and therefore do not measure the purity of the elements or have feelings at all. Individuals are mortal. The toxic remnants of institutional progress in the water and in breast milk are incalculable among institutional agendas. Is physically taxing pollution not reason enough to take inaction? Are the immediate, constant and plentiful problems from pollution not enough reason for pause? Many of the chemicals in our blood did not exist until recently; their long term effects are unknown. Is it not a crime to perpetuate pollution for profit by any means necessary, even at the cost of future life?

It is seemingly impossible to stop supporting the energy and oil corporations, but it is possible. It is possible to use well-founded, currently subjugated, alternatives. It is impossible to exit the environment, no matter how much the culture of separation would suggest, but it is possible and occasionally practical to leave institutions.

Under institutions, people become shells of their former selves. They make decisions on behalf of the institutions they are in and not considering the individuals they are among. Those inside institutions normally will not notice the rattling destruction the institution makes, just as being on the street can make it difficult to see the smog covering the cityscape.

When institutions hinder more than help, they should be removed or remade. But the actuality of institutional performance matters less, relative to what people believe about them. Walk out of institutions that exploit and pollute physicality and you. Institutions are nothing without the support of individuals and when they no longer benefit us and our surroundings, they should be eliminated or bettered without need for grief, for they are only formations, not life. Grieve for the dodo bird not some institution.

Institutions are not individuals, but they are made of and dependent on people. Doing the right thing is difficult, but it starts with stopping wrong. When wrong continues, it buries and blights the right, but as soon as wrongdoing ceases, what is right may blossom like spring flowers after a deluge. Think localization, not globalization. Stop buying globalized plastic crap. Supporting Chinese craftsmanship and artistry is righteous, whereas supporting Chinese oligarchies, supports the gentrification of Tibet, the pollution of China and the world and a pyramid system where the wealthy possess practically everything and the poor work practically all the time. China has such strict institutions, workers have been known to spend 16 hours a day at a factory, every day, for weeks at a time, behind locked doors in facilities so strict bathroom breaks are regulated.

On May Day, May 1, 1886, workers in the U.S.A. protested for rights and the 8 hour work day. As many as 80,000 people participated in a march in Chicago. Similar and subsequent strikes were carried out all over the U.S.A. Around 350,000 people across the U.S.A. participated in a general strike that went on for days. On May 3, Chicago police opened fire on protesters, killing four. On May 4, the protests continued. In Haymarket Square, Chicago, tensions peaked when police ordered the protesters to disperse. A bomb was thrown at the officers, they retaliated, firing indiscriminately, killing four protesters, six fellow officers and wounding an unknown number.

Without evidence seven men were later convicted of involvement in the bombing. The bomb tossed on May 4, 1886, was thrown by an unknown individual, but on November 11, 1887, four men were hung. The night before the execution a fifth killed himself with dynamite. Years later, in 1893, the Governor of Illinois pardoned the men who remained in prison and stated that the jury was essentially rigged and the men were victims of hysteria. Many unions and companies began adopting the eight hour work day and many laws were subsequently passed in favor of improved labor conditions. Yet only in 1938, was the eight hour work day entirely implemented with the Fair Labor Standards Act.

The Haymarket Square Protests illustrate a certain Master and Slave confrontation. During this revolution to promote the eight hour work day apparent infiltrators lit bombs in attempts to subvert the slave revolution. The protest for an eight hour work day, something we now take for granted required a national and global movement of individuals with a simple, quantifiable declaration. After the bombs the movement for an eight hour work day was temporarily slowed, but the wall the provocateurs built with violence couldn't stop the changing tide. Individual and mass consciousness developed despite the havoc.

There is now a written right to an eight hour work day in the U.S.A. There is now no more overt slavery or restrictions based on your skin color or heritage, now anyone of 18 can vote, including women, now anyone has the right to go where they want, say what they want and gather together to protest what they want, in theory anyway, as presented in the First Amendment. And yet if we are not opening up we are closing in.

"Gentlemen of the jury, convict these men, make an example of them, hang them and you save our institutions, our society." ~Julius Grinnell, Chicago Prosecutor

"The white man knows how to make everything, but he does not know how to distribute it." ~Sitting Bull

There are many lessons to be learned from the May 1886 protests as well as from looking at any protest or movement and reaction it causes. If there is a protest and you're a police officer, don't use force to break up the gathering because more protesters will come and if you shoot gathered people, you might kill them and fellow officers. Shootings and violence only feeds confrontation; it is only going to make people angry and protest ultimately more likely. Killing loses the moral authority and will eliminate support one may have had and gather more for opposition.

If you are a protester don't bring a bomb or any other means of violence to the protest. And make sure no agent provocateurs do either. When violence is unused and self-defense is prepared, done solely with the self, moral authority is kept and the cause expands. Be ready for violence though, because authorities are often assembled solely to use their boots and sticks. The legitimate authorities will wield their power along with illegitimate powers as well. And occasionally someone will throw bomb just to blame and degrade the protesters.

If peace is met with violence, there are always options other than fighting or fleeing and there are many ways to fight and many ways to flee. If peaceful protests are countered with violent institutions peaceful resolve is the answer. Violence perpetuates stagnancy and more violence. Revolutionaries have to retaliate with the destruction or building of symbols.

Peace and nonviolence are symbolic and revolutionary in the netherworld oligarchy. Peaceable assembly and stopping may be the most powerful form of resistance to the netherworld oligarchy, while violence and war are the oldest tools to maintain it. Machines do not require active dismantling, to stop them they might just be left alone. The same goes for institutions, walk away and they falter.

When institutions want to prevent a movement, the institutions label people violent or destructive or somehow contrary to the accepted culture of separation. Sometimes this takes place in complicated plots to implicate the peaceful. Sometimes it is done by committing violence on them and then presenting their self defense as attack. If they can turn peace to violence, they will. Institutions use violence in order to elevate their control, no matter if violence impedes betterment of individual situations. Some historians speculate that the person who threw the Haymarket Square bomb was an agent provocateur possibly working for steel corporations that had a lot to lose if workers gained rights.

All protests, strikes and stoppages are based on individuals and normally are based on calling attention to institutional violations. Political protests are made up of people from the lower and pressurized levels of the pyramid reacting to manipulations by those above. When many on one row protest and stop, change may occur. When a significant portion of a row, or small parts of many rows remove themselves the pyramidal structure is rattled. And if just a few of the bottom row move the whole system requires attention.

The words separation, abolish, and dissolve appear in the Declaration of Independence. It is a proclaimed departure from exploitation, a declaration of discontinuance of institutional support, a fuck you letter of the highest order. Stopping is perhaps the most powerful form of nonviolent action. The controlling institution's harsh reaction to peaceful protest is what normally leads to violent reaction and frequently that is what they want to instigate.

"Force, no matter how concealed, begets resistance." ~Lakota proverb

Regardless of the outcome and difficult shift, it is possible to cease participation in exploitation. Regardless of global power, it is possible to dismantle exploitative institutional architecture. Even if they are part of a company that works for royalty claiming correspondence with God, if wrong is the result, ceasing support actively rejects without confrontation. To stop wrong is the right thing and is increasingly, the necessary thing.

Global dimming is a consequence of the particulate from burning fuels being ejected into the atmosphere. Airborne particulate blocks sunlight and has a cooling effect. This is not a balancing act with global warming where everything works out. Global dimming does not equalize and stabilize warming. The combination makes the detriment less noticeable, until theoretically, an environmental tipping point is reached. Stop, you never know what you might find out. In fact scientists verified global dimming after 9/11 when air traffic over the U.S.A. ceased and noticeable changes occurred.

Another Northeast Indian legend with the transformative hero Gluscabi reveals what happens when we try to control and interfere with things we shouldn't. Gluscabi decides to go fishing, but the wind is too strong and he cannot paddle where he wants. He asks his grandmother where the wind comes from and she tells him about an eagle who makes the wind with his wings. Gluscabi marches into the wind and climbs a mountain to find the eagle. The wind from the eagle is so strong all of Gluscabi's hair is blown off him and he nearly falls off the mountain. Gluscabi tricks the eagle calling him granfather and ties him up. He then marches home to go fishing, but finds that it's now too hot to fish. He marches back to the mountain with his hair regrown and this time calls the eagle uncle and frees him. The eagle thanks him and calls him grandson. There are some things we should not stir up or tie and if we do we should do our best to remedy the situation, not ignore it.

To stop and declare independence from wrongdoing is the best way to resist without violence. To change, one must climb immense heights and often one must climb back and do it again. It is passive resistance. It is not passive-aggression, which is in part rooted in fear; it is standing up to wrongdoing without fear, peacefully. Stopping is difficult to manipulate because it is outside the status quo. Stop. Take a moment to look and listen, you never know what you might learn.

Murphy's Law is the notion stating anything that can go wrong will go wrong or if there is more than one way to do something, and one way will result in disaster, someone will do it that way and every precaution should be taken to prevent it. Edward Murphy was an aerospace engineer who is credited with originating the phrase, but it's an old sentiment and perhaps originally describing predicaments of ships at sea instead of components of flight.

Murphy's Law states what can go wrong will go wrong, and probably will go wrong at the least opportune moment, when one is farthest from shore. But

Murphy's Law is only the negative portion of a much older law, of a much older secret.

The secret behind Murphy's Law is not what may break, will break at the worst time. Overtly Murphy's Law considers the worst case scenarios and takes action to prevent them. If one does not consider prevention, one will face problems unprepared. And if one considers possibilities, one can eliminate hubris, the biggest killer next to curiosity.

"A danger foreseen is half-avoided." ~Cheyenne proverb

Before heading out to sea, considerations are made if the ship is sturdy and if the direction is worthy. But the secret is much more than that. Knowing what could break and then preventing it is the obvious lesson of Murphy's Law. Knowledge of what can happen is the precursor to the real secret.

When you know negative something is possible, you can prevent it and when you know something positive is possible you can actualize it. The secret is not limited to - what can happen, will happen. The secret is also what you will can happen. Every invention is first imagination. That which you will is possible and more likely the more you will it. The whole institutionalization of the military industrial complex all began as a thoughts manifest from will. Alternatively our will can stop its violent mechanics.

Murphy's Law most always refers to negative occurrences. This is only part of the truth, for what can happen is possibly positive just as easily can be willed to happen. When things go wrong people notice more, thus Murphy's Law, but the secret is constantly in effect. What can go right will go right at the most opportune moment too, if you will it. Mentally will it, and it will be. The real secret behind Murphy's Law precedes the name Murphy.

The secret is conscious actualization. Manifested actuality begins with imagination and idea, whether it's sailing through troubled waters or actualizing invention. Mind over matter is all a matter of mind. Information is powerful in part because of perspective that influences the mind to think negatively or positively, empowered or coward. Murphy's Law limits the secret. Information and open observation enables one to better understand and influence actuality. Perspective alone creates the ability to will new possibilities.

Knowledge not only recognizes actuality and possibility, but serves to expand possibility as well. Stopping diffuses corrupt machines and the most complicated institutional exploitation. The power to manifest begins with a seed, a thought. The power to change begins with stopping, with the construction and destruction of symbols.

"I do not believe in a fate that falls on men however they act, I do believe in a fate that falls on them unless they act."
Buddha

(Congress shall make no law respecting...right to peaceably assemble to)... petition the Government for a redress of grievances.

If institutions will not bend then action ensues. Revolutionary actions are nonviolent, noteworthy, and frequently noisy. The main requirement of revolutionary action is nonviolence for the status quo is the completely violent netherworld oligarchy. The martial formation of the world must be countered and there is nothing more revolutionary to violence than peaceful action. Peaceable assembly was revolutionary when the First Amendment was written and is revolutionary today, in a world gone mad with materialism controlled by martial institutionalism. The best peaceful action becomes a statement that raises awareness, the construction and destruction of symbols to instigate consciousness of actuality. Peaceful action can equally be bringing about benevolent processes to help people or action to cease the harm of people.

Revolution has to be nonviolent for the world is violent and revolution has to be pro-individual because the world is pro-institution. Revolutionary action has to be made of inarguable denouncement of a formation in the status quo so totally martial and oligarchical that no decently knowledgeable and decently compassionate person would disagree with the call to redress. But people tend to practice traditional bias as it concerns their national/political affiliation, their religion or their corporation. This traditional bias lends to support of the netherworld oligarchy over compassionate individuals. Revolutionary actions, whether handing out papers, standing on a soap box, protesting, or boycotting, or performing an institutional shutdown are so powerful that institutions will set up laws and strategies to prevent them from happening at all. And when such peaceful actions, peaceful rebellion, true American traditionalism is met with reactionary violence the movement is pressurized. Violent reactions often result from peaceful actions because it shines a light on the problem and people tend to attack the messenger. However institutions and individuals that react to peaceable protests with violence gain transparency and lose legitimacy. The violence is meant to scare away the masses from the signification of the construction and destruction of symbols.

Action causes reaction, if the reaction or effect one seeks is a violent one, violence is enacted, for violence is a likely result of violence. If one wants outcomes other than violence, one must perform actions other than violent ones, like construction and destruction of symbols. When there is a violent reaction to peaceful protests and gatherings, it is to destroy the movement's expansion through fear. The violence is to instill fear or retaliation. The intentions behind violence are to intimidate and eliminate, or to instigate and discredit. If people do not back down and do not violently retaliate, violence might be diffused and overcome. If such violence is met with courage, the movement gathers more attention and momentum. The revolutionaries must disobey immoral laws, exploitive laws and laws diffusing the First Amendment, but must be nonviolent.

Do something daring, creative, wild and nonviolent in order to stop exploitation and violence. If there is not a little green revolution Earth Mother will continue to be degraded. In order to instigate change do something alternative. To instigate revolution, do something revolutionary, think r-evolutionary. To counter the pyramid system requires countering pyramidal formation. To initiate real change, alternative systems or shapes are instigated instead of simply countering oppositions.

Simply stopping is a change and a powerful action toward further change. If enough people stop together, it results in rapid change. But sometimes stopping may not be enough; more accurately sometimes there may not be enough people who stop together. There were many protests concerning the new tea policies, before the Boston Tea Party, but they did not garner the attention needed to make a difference. The destructive night of civil disobedience destroyed corporate product. It was an act meant to communicate. The Boston Tea Party made sure to make and keep distinction between the destructive act of civil disobedience, the noblest defiance and any possibility it could be mistaken for theft.

If there are unanswered questions on exploitation, enact civil disobedience. Disrupt the status quo to instigate the investigation of exploits and the evolution of liberty among the 85%. All forms of nonviolent protest are rooted in discontinuance. If one wants change, one finds alternatives and discontinues support of the status quo.

The First Amendment is made up of five rights, and also presents a prescription of to keep rights. They work together as well as by themselves. Many successful revolutions followed the five rights of revolution in order, but depending on the specifics one can use them all at once or in any combination.

Perhaps the most powerful form of revolution, the most productive, inarguable and non-injurious is stopping. Active discontinuance of performance for institutions disables them. To boycott and cease support of an exploitive institution and let everyone know is the most powerful, nonviolent and inarguable act to initiate change and ease the steep slant of the pyramidal system.

If individuals, who otherwise support an institution boycott instead, the institution crumbles or changes. If individuals boycotted multiple exploitive institutions, the foremost superfluous institutions would fall by the wayside soonest. The most unsustainable elements of the pyramid would reveal their structural instability right away. Those institutions that are actually needed would remain and the most useless of them would transform into vacant space.

"My young men shall never work, men who work cannot dream; and wisdom comes to us in dreams. You ask me to plow the ground. Shall I take a knife and tear my mother's breast? Then when I die she will not take me to her bosom to rest. You ask me to dig for stone. Shall I dig under her skin for bones? Then when I die I cannot enter her body to be born again. You ask me to cut grass and make hay and sell it and be rich like white men. But how dare I cut off my mother's hair? ~Smohalla, founder of the dreamer religion, Sokulk band of Nez Perce

Money has a grip on many, but can provide a powerful grasp as well. One person with a million dollars could possibly change the world, but even better is one million people with one dollar. One person can eventually build a structure, but many can make a better structure at exponential speed. The same is true concerning the dismantling or remaking of a structure.

If enough people decided to live using significantly less power until the grid sharply increased its solar and renewable energy sources, energy providers might scramble to find a way to get your money. They would suddenly figure out a cheap and easy way to install solar panels on some sunny properties already attached to the grid. Many institutions endorse the statement that free energy is expensive to initiate. This maybe so, but to whom is free energy expensive?

The privileges institutions hold could be canceled by simply abandoning their systems. Institutions crumble when they lose the support of money and mentality. It is good to boycott to change now and then even if they are not necessarily diabolical. Among other reasons, it reminds those who think they are in control that at any time people can shake their foundations. Institutions despise change partly because if they didn't make it happen or let it happen, they don't gain from it.

If people are suddenly without their wants, there might be volatility, but people adjust. If suddenly needs were unavailable, there might be chaos, but people adapt. Problem solving through questions turns new problems into new solutions. Individuals are adaptable, not institutions. Most institutions are not based on our future needs, but our present wants.

"Be satisfied with the needs instead of the wants." ~Sioux saying

If institutions are faced with options where they would either lose a lot or be eliminated, they might change. But first they would try to hold on and maintain in institutionalized format. Institutions are not adaptable. They are maintainable, like all machines. Institutions develop, but largely institutions act to maintain situations rather than progress them.

Many institutions are capable of goodness. And yet they also exploit regionally in order to reap reward. The larger the institution the worse they are; the oil corporations power the war machines and the war machines power the oil corporations; one supports the other. Institutions cannot stop, they are not made to stop; people have to stop. Institutions are all like nuclear power generation experiments, a chain reaction that must be stopped, that cannot stop itself.

Institutions in the netherworld oligarchy confuse people and attempt to strip people of their instinct to question. What is the best action in any given situation? When a situation is questionable, one should begin by questioning it and proceed as the First Amendment prescribes as situations develop.

Powerlessness is a common sentiment among people today. This notion has perhaps never been more prevalent considering the power that people do wield, the information at their disposal. Information is power and it is plentiful. Despite all at our disposal, despite all of our responsibility and our complicity, people still believe they cannot counter the system in postmodernism, the era of institutional rule. People forget that the status quo is simply formations put into action by others. People can change.

Today activism must continue and stopping must begin. Movement and participation is essential to life. In the era of institutionalization, inactivism and withdraw is more powerful and perhaps always was more than any alternative protest against exploitation. Declaring independence and discontinuance is, at times, essential to life, liberty and the pursuit of happiness. Think of sit ins or Occupy. Stopping holds ground and institutions want you to keep moving on their paths.

Inactivism implies laziness to those who are committed to their path, to those against stopping wrongdoing. It actually takes tremendous effort to stop and leave the status quo, to stop performing wrongs they claim are for toward some greater right. In the era of institutionalization, wrong is abundant, intermixed in physicality and mentality as pollution and misinformation. If one lacks persistent questioning one might consume or produce poisons without knowing it.

The pollution in the era of institutionalization is inescapable. There is no silent oasis, no place left undisturbed. Everywhere is tainted no matter how distant from humanity. Petrol and its toxic accompaniments are in the waters of deep wells and in the high reaches of the atmosphere as well. The background levels of radiation have been steadily rising since the inception of the nuclear era everywhere. Genetic alteration of plants and animals has taken place with irreversible consequences. There is no vacating the petrolithic era and nuclear age, there is no going back, but one can still cease and evict exploitation. There is no going backwards, but you can act.

If institutions or individuals argue against stopping wrong, you know that they are wrong, dependent on wrong, and that there is probably something wrong with them. Stopping wrong becomes more essential as the era of institutionalization continues to expand. When institutions and individuals argue over stopping wrongdoing that directly and negatively effects life on the planet, you know something is seriously wrong with them.

Many scientists refer to the end of the twenty-first century as the beginning of the sixth mass extinction of the planet. A majority also believe it may be the fastest rate of extinction, eclipsing even the sudden doom of the dinosaurs, the last mass extinction. Earth Mother, the planet's sensitive ecosystem we are dependent on for our breath, water, life and depth of thought is being dismantled, disfigured and destroyed for institutions. The gardens of the Earth are disappearing and with them, all that people take for granted.

The ability to question and answer is the distinguishing characteristic of man. Other beings have heart and mind and can feel and think, but they cannot question and manipulate an answer into being like man. Questioning is both the result of evolution and surely the very instigation of it. Thinking is God's gift to people that makes hands useful. The lion has cunning, teeth and claws; man has reasoning, voice and hands.

The use five rights of revolution is a revolutionary's primary means to counter the oligarchical era of institutionalization and should be celebrated. The prescription for individual revolution, The First Amendment, is in fact stomped on by institutions throughout the world. To question and dissect the intricacy of the simple apple and the complex universe is our right and our divinity. However, there is no need to question the distinction of right and wrong, it just is. There are no ifs, ands or buts about it. There are certain acts and instants that are always wrong. Violence is wrong. Exploitation is wrong. Environmental destruction is wrong. Slavery is wrong. Withholding, distorting or otherwise tampering with information and the truth is wrong. Bringing harm to others and impeding on the liberty of others is wrong.

The components of the status quo tend to be wrong. Revolutionary individuals lean toward what is right and today that alone becomes revolutionary. Everything is questionable. In the petrolithic era and nuclear age stopping increasingly is necessary in order to continue. Stop or be stopped. To discontinue, to stop and to become an inactivist as much as possible, with as many others as possible, is the way to change the status quo. Stopping proves to everyone, to individuals and institutions that people hold the power. Active stopping is the most powerful action for a revolution, for change.

To walk away from the mass of wrong that is the pyramid system of the status quo is the best form to fight it and dismantle it. It is fighting without fighting. Stop buying new cars. Stop using power for a day. Stop war permanently. Leave the left wing and the right wing of the status quo and walk off, let the BS bird fly away. The new world, the era of institutionalization requires a new kind of activism - inactivism. Stop following serpents on institutionalized branches.

Forget working for, and in the format of their sham, which forever promises future benefit and permanently provides present headache. Forget lining up to round up all that is around in order to capitalize and construct a pyramid of capitalization within and according to the status quo. Stop temporarily, partially or permanently.

The environmental conditions of the petrolithic era and nuclear age call for stopping. Individuals are capable of adjustment and of adaptation to great variants. Individuals are capable of stopping and an assortment of other spontaneous, frivolous or serious actions. Actions derived from a colorful assortment of interests, including, but not limited to, stopping and starting off in a different direction. And in the U.S.A. as long as one doesn't impede or traverse over others in the process, charge or pause, in liberty.

People are capable of numerous accomplishments, but perhaps our highest functions, as individuals, is our ability to meditate and dance, to be still and contemplate and to dance for celebration. Institutions cannot mimic our higher levels of being, institutions cannot meditate and cannot have fun. Institutions are not designed to stop and contemplate or move in a frivolous manner for they are not living.

Consideration of totality goes counter to institutional agendas. Institutions continue, in order to grow and monopolize as tolerations permit and they need you to do it. Institutions are not alive and have no heart, yet they present Ronald McDonald personas that seem immortal and inspire people to adopt a second, fake heart. There is no way to continue at this rate of consumption and pollution, but institutions would herald otherwise according to their limited contemplations. Institutions would have you continue down their path instead of ever meditating or dancing.

Earth Mother may not thrive as much as before thanks to the instigation of the era of institutionalization, thanks to our activities, but the era of institutionalization must be stopped by choice or it will be ceased without choice. Peaceful resistance, nonparticipation and non-cooperation with institutional wrongdoing are the best ways to dismantle the netherworld oligarchy and heal Earth Mother. To implement right first stop wrong, it is inarguable by way of any logic. Only wendigos and two hearts would perpetuate wrongdoing.

Laws have been made and broken in the evolution of ideas, sometimes laws have to be broken. Legality does do not necessarily correlate with morality. Sometimes laws must be broken so people see the wrong of the law. There are many defiant and heroic acts that were also criminal. Violence defeats ideas whereas nonviolence uplifts ideas, even a laws are broken in the process. Nonviolent inaction is directly, inevitably, universally and inarguably, now, then and later on, the most powerful and inarguable form of activism. Stopping is a powerful statement and it is earsplitting to institutions when choursed with coherent numbers holding their space.

Inactivists commit no wrong, and yet could change the world with a week of meditation or dance or any distraction other than the continuation of wrong within the netherworld oligarchy. In a week or month of discontinuance the world would change. Instead of historical events constantly consisting of war, people could carry out a worldwide year of peace and cease, a worldwide event more notable than any battle or bloodletting institutions have ever heralded, a mark on the timeline grander than all the scars of every war, a healing.

Globalization eliminates localization and instigates exploitation. War is institutionally engaged and managed, but individuals fight it. Both war and pollution from globalization have to be implemented by individuals. Institutions are not designed to cease, they last lifetimes without ever pausing. War is a temporary adjustment for many institutions, a planned disruption that many benefit from. However for people it can be a permanent disembarkation. A stoppage, a protest, inactivism is peaceful war on institutions. Peaceful inactivism, in meditation and dance, destroys institutions as war destroys individuals.

"With all things and in all things, we are relatives." ~Sioux saying

Sometimes, it takes a criminal act to demonstrate that the entire philosophy behind the act being illegal is wrong. But as soon as people get hurt, even accidentally, the voice is belittled, the point is dulled and instead of protest or statement crime is interpreted. One cannot be violent and expect to communicate a message, even if that violence is accidental, even if that violence is towards you.

Animals are capable of vicious violence, but man even without technological advantage is capable of more tireless violence than all the animal kingdom. At the same time, a distinction of man among animals, is the ability to act and react in nonviolent capacity, we all have the distinct ability to help and heal. Revolution in the netherworld oligarchy can begin with simply doing the latter as developed consciousness vehicles.

Violence in the name of any cause profits strangers, particularly the strangers who manufacture and fuel weaponry. Violence, despite any reason presented, is in the interest of institutional control. The first electrical impulse and reaction may be to fight or take flight, but there are always other options and both of these are fear based. Fight or flight is perhaps the archetypal primordial choice. It is our initial frightful reaction to situations from the reptilian brain, but there are always other choices and there are always more ways to fight and take flight than strike or run. In that first instant of processing information it might seem like the only choice, but finding other options enables progression.

Nelson Mandela was imprisoned for a lifetime. Countless unnamed people have been imprisoned for breaking the law and doing the right thing at the same time. People who stand up and face wrong, without fighting or fleeing, offering peaceful resistance, are always in the right.

People who are tossed inside a box for peaceful resistance and then break their cage asunder are always right, no matter what is broken getting out of the cage. Revolutionaries stand up, speak up and if need be, act up, no matter the legality, for revolutionaries deal in morality. Revolutionaries follow the five rights of revolution described in the First Amendment.

Thomas Edison came up with a lot of ideas. On top of numerically conceptualizing the thinking community in his 85%, 10% and 5% articulation Thomas had well over one thousand patents on his inventions among them were improvements to alkaline batteries for electric automobiles. Before petrol became standard electric vehicles were commonplace and Thomas believed they were the best option. He invested a decade of work into improving electric batteries for vehicles, but by the time he finished, the electric starter made petrol powered vehicles more acceptable. Thomas was a great thinker. He is best known for recognizing the formula to make the light bulb work; however someone else already had the formula. Thomas invented many things besides the carbon filament for light bulbs, but Joseph Swan originally came up with that idea.

Thomas is known to have sat at his desk in contemplation of mechanical concepts for hours at a time. Albert Einstein is known to have similarly sat contemplatively, only sober. He would sit at his desk, high on opium, studying a certain problem and during his inquisitive stupor he would hold ball bearings in one hand. As his sedation grew and eventually he would pass out at his desk and the instant Thomas fell asleep the ball bearings fell onto the wood floor, waking him. He induced the dream state to enhance and stimulate his mind then woke himself up to variously flash upon ideas.

In the dream state the mind has much higher cognitive abilities than usual. It was not the opium, though Thomas may have believed so, it is us. When we first fall asleep, we enter the dream state and engage a different, more aware mind state. In the dream state, the entirety of the dreamscape is understood for it is all via your own mind. In the dream state we are capable of accessing what is known as the Akashic Field or the universal consciousness and knowing intuitively.

"All dreams spin out from the same web." ~Hopi saying

In that moment when you first enter the dream state, your mind is ready and willing to understand entirety, intoxicated or not. The mind is accustomed to opening up and making all comprehensible, including the intricate functions of machinery. As we fall into deeper sleep we become less lucidly in control, but in the transitional state we can find great insights.

Thomas would sleep on it, for just an instant. This brilliance is available to us all. Instead of a lucid dream, when you know it's a dream and are in control, this is more lucid reality, when you know you are awake, but comprehend reality as if it were your dream. The transitional state between awake and sleep can lead to great invention.

This state is apparently more attainable in the moment, when you first fall asleep and are gently awakened, though it's possible to experience the meditative effects variously. One relaxes, concentrates and falls sleep, at the same time. It's much easier to reap the benefit of the dream state when you then wake up. In order to benefit from the dream state focus on one thing, relax completely, and shift consciousness. Sometimes the sooner one wakes up after shifting to sleep the more likely you will have such an intuitive experience. Opiates or drugs are not a requirement. By doing this practice one is able to pull ideas from the mind in a dream state and not from a mind state in a dream. The answer is within.

"Sometimes dreams are wiser than waking." ~Black Elk

To initiate action, one must be correct and safe. One must coordinate every aspect and prevent every onset of violence or mishap. If any individual is hurt, the activist's message is potentially lost. People will wonder what is wrong with the purveyors of violence and not what they were trying to say. To discontinue, to stop is the simplest and most powerful course to change. It is the most powerful and loudest action that hurts only those who are dependent on wrong. Stopping wrongdoing rocks the boat and exposes the wrong to the unquestioning majority, the 85%. Stopping wrong reveals wrong, it does no wrong. Stopping provides the 85% with glimpses of actuality, instigating questioning a different direction. By stopping, there is ending and by ending, there can be beginning.

If cemented wrongdoing is ceased there might be repercussions, rattling and shaking. There will be spoiled vegetables when people refuse to eat genetically modified food or individuals might go hungry. Institutions will blame such on inactivists and not the institutionalization, integration of wrongdoing. Right now individuals are suffering, directly, because we are not stopping. Change is frightening, but the institutional status quo leads to suffering. Continuation of the status quo is rattling to the environment and the happiness of individuals, conclusion is dangerous and rattling to institutions. Stop what is wrong, regardless of the consequences. Institutions continue to build the netherworld oligarchy regardless of the consequences. Which is more acceptable? Which is more dangerous?

Freedom is the freedom to do the math and question their math. Question your own doubt of holding the answers, and more importantly, question the surety of others who provide answers. To cease wrong hurts no individual, but it does make institutions shudder, crack and change. To cease is peaceful and presents power to people. No farmer should stop growing, but they should stop growing GMO. No doctor should stop healing, but they should stop supporting pharmaceutical corporations. Healers should question homeopathic and allopathic treatment and not simply refer to regimented procedures.

Stopping participation in wrong, no matter the outcome, is never wrong. When there is negative result from simply stopping wrong, it is because of the integration of wrong, not the action taken to call attention to it. When there are negative results from ceasing wrong it is because of the institutionalized dependency on wrong.

To stop wrong, stop wrong. There is no complete disconnect from the Wendigo world, it is here and will be here for the foreseeable future. There is virtually no strata that has escaped the consequences of the claws. It is impossible to bring back the pristineness of Earth Mother entirely, there is no going back, but it is possible to stop wrong and start healing. The most powerful way to start anything is to stop first, and in this case ceasing support of institutional wrongdoing. One cannot separate oneself from Earth Mother, but it's possible and powerful to disconnect from institutions. Negative consequences of change are often the only thing noticed, but stopping wrong is inarguably not wrong. Blaming those who stop, is worse than blaming messengers for sharing information, it's like blaming the caterpillar for pausing to cocoon.

Institutions of the netherworld oligarchy try to stop protests, because protests stop institutions. Since the Occupy Wall Street movement it became a felony to annoy police in New York State and illegal to wear a mask to a protest in Canada. Ceasing participation in wrongdoing is the most inarguable and powerful reaction to wrongdoing; fighting it fuels it. The most powerful action is the lack thereof. Refuse to move, stop. The best way to restore natural balance in a world overwhelmed by institutionalized wrong, is to simply stop. Wrong can only be accomplished with constant maintenance.

Behind the Wall

Hopi tradition states this is the fourth world or fourth age of this world. All the ages experience birth, growth, entropy and death. The idea is similar to the Yugas, an ancient Hindu presentation and understanding of time where we are in the fourth age, the least perfect realm. There was the age of truth, age of mostly truth, age of little truth and the kali yuga, the age of mostly lies.

The Hopi creation story of this world begins as the last world was ending in some nonspecific calamity. A few people were taken underground, saved by ant people. The ant people took our ancestors underground and taught us how to survive, how to grow food and hide from disaster. Eventually people returned aboveground to and were told to walk the four directions and reunite.

At first the creation story such seems like many indigenous tales, but comparatively and allegorically speaking the Hopi creation story approaches perfection in its eloquence. Ants are the only animal in the world that humanity can be accurately compared with so much so that perhaps mankind was influenced by ants more than any other being. Humans and ants are farmers, warriors, harvesters, thieves and enslavers alike. No other animal behaves like man, except ants, no other being is as warmongering. Individually we each might be more like a dog or cat, or perhaps we might like to see ourselves as similar in character to a bird, but as a collective mankind is like antkind.

Human history in total, from whatever nationalistic, religious or otherwise jingoistic perspective one endures can be read like the proud Argentine Ant's recital of the invasion of New Orleans and California. The Argentine Ant spent millions of generations building up not only defensive structure, but amassing invasion forces to take over as much of South America as antly possible. Any other ant colony they encounter they destroy. They vanquish all other antkind and if they believe anything they believe they are the chosen ant. Ants are extremely intelligent if intelligence is measured in utilizing surroundings as tools. The Argentine Ant grew accustomed to hopping on floating leaves or debris in the Argentine flood plains and hitching rides downstream to effectively expand their territory. They were such mighty warriors with such rich resources that no other ant could challenge them.

When steamships began embarking from Argentinian shores they carried with them invasion force after invasion force of the chosen ants. Wherever the ship was steered the ants embarked and began total and complete annihilation of all other ants and competitive life. The chosen ants have now formed a global collective. The megacolony of god's chosen ant superpower has conquered California, Japan, and most of the Mediterranean and they are right now, on the march. Interestingly enough, the Argentine Ants recognize and accept each other no matter what continental colony they are from, and destroy all others.

"Societies with population explosions, that extend into the millions, are prone to large-scale, intense, tactical warfare. It's a nature of battle only possible among communities with plenty of excess labor force." Mark Moffet

Ants and humans have virtually no societal limit to their growth. The environment limits their growth, not their instincts or biological needs. Few other species on the planet operate in this manner. The colony be hundreds, or millions or billions. No other species have societies of this proportion and no other animal behaves the way ants and people do. No other species kills and enslaves each other and no other species practices complete confrontation in war like humans and ants.

The Argentine Ant megacolony has traversed the globe staking claim to significant areas on six continents. It is akin to human colonialism only the insect expansion and elimination is even more one sided. No other ant it seems can stand up to the Argentine Ants. On the borders of the new intercontinental megacolonies are ant wars of total annihilation where all fall to the Argentine Ant's fierceness.

Human history is exactly like the history of a more prideful ant colony, only mammalian with opposable thumbs. People are the aboveground version of ants with internal skeletons instead of external ones, with hands and vocal chords instead of antennae and mandible crushers. And instead of being capable of lifting great weight like ants people are capable of inventing great machines.

Within the colony the queen lives for decades. Workers live for years. And the expendable males live for a matter of weeks. Nests might have a history of multiple queens. But the colony at large has a rich history of millions of years and acts with the impetus of such an age old regime. They are biologically reinforced matriarchies with a history that makes the rise of humanity just another pulse of different beings to eat off, with different kinds of leaves to ride.

Ants farm, they harvest from their surroundings, they enslave and steal from other ants and they war on each other. Perhaps the most amazing similarity between man and ant is the fact that we build infrastructure for future use. Mankind and antkind build and we both build based largely on concerns for protection from each other, out of concern for war and others stealing from us. Ants build anthills and then build massive tunnels based on defense of the queen if enemy ants were to invade. Mankind builds in the same manner, as a means of protection.

"Oh Great Spirit who made all races, look kindly upon the whole human family and take away the arrogance and hatred which separate us from our brothers." ~Cherokee Prayer

Mankind and antkind function, as collectives, the same, only antkind came first. One can almost imagine a curious individual coming up with all sorts of ideas watching antkind build and behave. Perhaps the original pyramids and pyramid builders saw their structures as having antkind qualities, built in symbolic homage to the antkind structure and mindset, or perhaps they were unaware that their great buildings mimicked antkind's mounds. Typically instead of underground tunnel defenses man largely built perimeter defenses, though now we have built up walls of every sort. Now we have underground bases, built as protection from the enemy humans if they attack, but mostly mankind built walls as protection. Because of man's inventiveness walls are now largely technological as is our ability to confront each other. Mankind made armaments which could kill all other opposition and all other life in the process, including god's chosen ant. As our inventiveness in killing each other expanded mankind, effectively smarter ants with fingers, began building deeper underground putting protective walls and above. Both antkind and mankind build war culture and war structure. It is a celebrated shared tradition. And in

130

many ways what ill-informed people mistake to be art or culture is actually just symptomatic of the war machine's institutionalized control.

Ants and people are always prepared for war instead of being prepared for peace. And when the opportunity presents itself, because all preparations have been made, because the opposition is seemingly prepared or is not and therefore ought to be confronted or enslaved, war takes place. War takes place because it has been readied. At the borders of ant populations wars are taking place right now where millions are being killed every month. The ants kill each other because of their differences, despite the fact they are all ants. Humans when placed in bordered blocks suffer the same end, war based on differences despite our sameness. It is arguable that the predominant measure of distinction between people is differences in perception. But borders are volatile the same as with ants and man.

The most diverse human borders have always been places of the most hair-raising and antennae flickering wars, like the areas in France and elsewhere major fighting in WWI and WWII took place. A more intense example of the ant like nature of humanized borders is demonstrated throughout The Middle East. Multiple doctrines, including the one true religion, coincide with national differences, heritage distinctions and cultural fluctuations to form borders of all sorts. And war of all sorts. War is an inevitability for antkind and mankind if they decide to act like ants.

Humans differentiate each other for a variety of entirely absurd or historically valid reasons, if history is valid at all, but the result is the same -states with proud histories or colonies with biological impulses and the outsiders they clash with along the borders.

Humans are not so complicated for a human to understand, and we are all spurred by the same god or same forces that created ants. So perhaps it is not so difficult to understand which ant is best. It is whichever ant is able to develop and evolve, which so far, for the last 150 million years at least, they have not done much by the way of. It is perhaps an impulse from beyond the beyond to not only be tribal and build walls, but to war on each other. It must be an impulse for ants do not have minds as man does. No matter if one is a tiny robotic entity of an underground ant mound or a aware human, the pulse within to kill beings like you, but not like you enough, is biological, a wiring of earth.

Man is more complex than the old ant because of our complex inventions, most made toward and during war. Instead of antennae we have phones. Instead of claws and teeth we have knives and guns and nuclear bombs. We war on each other the same, we enslave each other the same, humans may have very well thought of agriculture in the first place by watching ants and building pyramids in the middle of our cities by watching ant colonies. Perhaps the Hopi were more correct than we could ever know. Perhaps long ago man was adopted by ants or at least adopted the ways of ants residing deep underground.

Ants were the world's first farmers. They effectively raise livestock too and harvest from their surroundings and such behavior began about 50 million years ago or more. Today many ants still farm or tend to fungus grown in their lairs for the colony to eat, harvesting plant material for the fungus to consume in turn. Some ants raise aphids for the colony cafeteria. One can almost envision a curious primal human ancestor watching ants do what they do and gaining numerous ideas, good, bad and ugly ideas.

Ants are the only other living thing to enslave others, the bigger ants takeover the smaller ants naturally. Or like the Argentine ants instead of enslaving they annihilate. Humanity's enslavement of weaker people is comparable to bigger ants meeting smaller ants. Violence and war however perverse is rooted in biological aspects proven by antkind and yet mankind discusses war as tradition, or societal formation, or economics, or politics. People present reasoning for killing each en masse, but it's biological response we are able to surpass, or would be if it were not institutionalized into society. If war politics were noted to be base thinking of lower life like that of anthood, people would simply attempt to surpass the biological response with alternative higher thinking.

Ants are the only animal that can accurately be compared to man, mainly because no other animals are as culturally developed with such refined caste systems and no other species kill each other on a massive organized scale. No other species wars. Mankind is more efficient at construction and destruction, we live a little longer, our colonies are more noticeable and impactful, we voyage to harvest and conquer and practices the same behavior as antkind comparable to them in our complexity, or our simplicity depending on you look at it.

The comparable harvesting, farming, raising of livestock, enslavement of other ants and war organization of antkind and mankind make us remarkably similar. Perhaps of all our shared traits the most detrimental similarity is the fact that antkind and mankind both build walls. Perhaps the fact that we build walls is actually the most markedly similar characteristic between us, initiating all other similarities. Perhaps the fact that we build walls and forts and prepare for war leads to the tendency to war and plunder those outside the walls in the first place. Perhaps the wall builders alone spurred the necessity to find tools as more efficient means of warring or plundering resources or building better forts. Ants and humans build complex dwellings in part as a way to defend the collective, which appears righteous, but it is primarily the result of the induced and near permanent individual mind state and collective physical state of war.

Humans have been practicing cultural traditions reminiscent of quality ant relationships for thousands of years. The reason humans are so good at building is because we are always at war. Humanity has been building walls literally and figuratively since the time of Han, Nehemiah and long before. Ants build holes and labyrinths and humans build underground too, but mainly humans built walls and towers. Man is the aboveground ant.

The Western Wall or Wailing Wall is an ancient wall of high symbolic significance –people have been killing each other at the base of walls for thousands of years. The Wailing Wall is sacred. The Great Wall of China is another physical line in the sand where people killed each other. The Great Wall is so great that it can be seen from space and everybody wants you to know that so that you think that walls are great, after all they can be seen from space. Teachers teach that walls are great. Walls are perimeters, borders, where war is readied and armament is installed and where the bordermind kicks in like that of all great ants.

It is easy to observe ants. We can observe their comings and goings and learn what they do over many lifetimes. Imagine observation of people as we would an ant hill or ant farm. Imagine we could watch the Wailing Wall or the Great Wall of China for a century or two. Imagine if we could watch what happened at the Berlin Wall during its comparatively brief existence. We would see the bordermind of antkind in mankind too.

Walls are an example of false pride. False pride results in the bordermind. An example of false pride is being proud of how you were born; what country you're from, the quantity of melanin you were born with or the things your ancestors did. Real pride, which even that should be let go, is having done something on your own. This false pride in walls built thousands of years ago is the same. Forget about the ancient walls and do something new with your hands. Walls have been getting in the way of the development of our collective mentality for millennia. Walls make us more like ants than farming or harvesting or raising livestock. Walls build up the infrastructure that maintains war and the mind state of war.

The complexity of antkind society might have more intricate functions, comparable to how mankind would like to see ourselves, than we would care to admit. Perhaps ants communicate and even individually think within the collective as we would like to think we are. As easy as we can observe antkind we can't really know how they are inside. But we can understand our own inner being.

Mankind builds physical walls for war to promote the bordermind in false pride. We also have the capability to build mental and spiritual walls and encase individuals and whole societies in such binds. The mental and spiritual binds and locks and encasements we are surrounded by hold us and entrap us just as walls do. And just like walls we believe the walls are protecting us when in fact they are perpetuating the mind state of war.

We are educated primarily within walls and informed of the greatness of the Great Wall. We are informed directly and indirectly as we grow up in the education system. We are taught outright about certain concepts and we learn other concepts indirectly. What the teacher teaches is one thing and how the system is formed is another thing altogether. As powerful individuals we conceive a learn and understand so many things that we often don't immediately calculate everything that we are taking in. Youthful and exuberant minds learn and perceive more than others do too. We learn from early on about all the great walls and great wars and great buildings people have erected. And while we're learning the history of mankind we learn to stay in line and shut up. We learn to zip it shut. We learn to seal ourselves up and barricade our mind and spirit closed to the rest of the world. We learn to conform at every angle by what we are taught and more importantly how we are taught.

We learn that how much we know matters little compared to how much we know about conforming to the status quo. We close ourselves in and make our own individual walls in order to protect us from others, leaving us stuck —with ourselves. The bordermind is initiated and we live encased in walls people spiritually and mentally put around us and that walls we built around ourselves. We are walled in by experiences which produce layers of façade and ego armor in individuals and a culture of separation among modern and post-modern society. We close ourselves in from reality in ways we shouldn't and try to in ways we couldn't.

No matter who is telling the story, whether Einstein or an American Indian elder, the valuable truths are eternally applicable. Questioning, seeking truth, is also eternally valuable. And so is ceasing cooperation with systems, which on questioning, prove to be wrongful and based on lies. Stopping wrong is an eternally applicable and valuable act. Stop, it leads to art and cultural development. Proactive focused inactivity spurs societal change and consciousness development of the individual and the collective.

Institutions are formed to control people, some of them are designed to control your very thinking while others control your very being. The very word government, arguably the oldest and most powerful type of institution, means rule the mind. Institutions seek to control, to rule the mind. And most institutions do so through as little as the presentation of information, through the omission of information. While governments do that and more. The overt functions of government design situations through promotion and prohibition. Governments promote and prohibit and whatever they promote or prohibit forms the collective.

"In politics, nothing happens by accident. If it happens, you can bet it was planned that way," ~Franklin D. Roosevelt

Institutions seek to control, the same then as now. The very old idea of the blood right of kings is rooted in oligarchic, dare I say parasitic tendency to seek control. But it's the same type of oligarchic, parasitic behavior representative of the modern day Supreme Court Institutions United decision to give First Amendment rights to corporate institutions.

The greatest problem today, as it was hundreds and perhaps even thousands of years ago, the root of all the world's ills, is the institutionalization of individuals and the polar accompaniment of the individuation of institutions. The individuation of institutions, like the blood right of kings and like the Supreme Court decision are made to make it easier to institutionalize individuals, like the etymological origins of the word government.

Institutions, government especially, promote and prohibit. As the old saying goes, 'The right hand halts and the left hand beckons.' Governments halt and beckon. Governments rule the mind through as little as distribution and restriction of information and as much as outright promotion and prohibition.

All government institutions operate in nearly the same way and many today are practically the same. As different as governments of the world are most promote and prohibit similarly. Nearly all governments of the world promote war and nuclear experimentation with the deadliest materials imaginable which kill and deform all life. At the same time nearly all governments prohibit production of hemp and consumption of marijuana which provide a narcotic equivalent to kava juice, or valerian root and an industrial powerhouse for quality food, clothing, shelter, curative medicine, etc. Nearly all the governments of the world promote the most dangerous materials imaginable, equitable only Pandora's Box and prohibit the most harmless and possibly most beneficial plants.

The contrast of which not only depicts the individuation of institutions, but also the institutionalization of individuals. Nuclear experimentation industry is given exceptions and special rights, while individuals are threatened with incarceration because of marijuana. In the U.S.A. the Price Anderson Act promoted nuclear experimentation, stating that any major nuclear experimentation catastrophes will be covered by the U.S.A. government. Otherwise no insurance company would talk with nuclear experimentation institutions that wanted to build and operate multiple nuclear water boilers next to each other. The Price Anderson Act promoted oligarchical institutions, literally at the cost of the environment and all in it.

The prohibition of marijuana has imprisoned generations and built up a police state. Since its implementation literally generations have been institutionalized because of an unaltered plant. While nuclear power plants and nuclear experimentation permanently have altered entirely. Today the vast majority of systems promote the individuation of institutions and the institutionalization of individuals, none so harshly as the promotion of nuclear experimentation and the prohibition of hemp and marijuana cultivation.

Nuclear experimentation is the most harmful and costly promotion any government could ever possibly enact, while in contrast prohibition of marijuana and hemp is perhaps most harmful and costly prohibition enacted by any government. That's why I'm with the 99%. Because institutions predominantly promote and prohibit systems any conscious individual would stand up against. Institutions are not individuals my friend. They never have been and never will be.

Sometimes language itself will build up walls mentally and spiritually around us. Predominantly through the direct and indirect learning via institutions and institutionalization individuals learn what they should reject and consider and what we should do and seek through subtle language instruction and suggestion. The presentation of everything depends on language. Perhaps because people do not lack antennae to determine reality through chemical and pheromone detection instead of having to verbally determine how much or how little one is being lied to. Since mankind cannot detect the pheromones and electrical impulses as easily as antkind we have to discern lies through vocalization and body language. Mankind requires experience to determine lies. The best way to develop on the experience required to detect lies is to ask questions. Ask questions when you think people are lying, ask question when you think they are not lying and ask from the perspective opposite to what you hold or of no perspective. Observe how people answer your questions when asked with the perspective that you believe them and when you don't and when you are apparently being just curious. Look into people's eyes and also look their overall presence. Practice doing so when it is not serious so that the next time the matter is serious and people are being lead in the wrong direction you might be able to better discern and call out the lies.

We are crowded in and often misinformed by our own experiences too. We are trained, in ways we don't realize, to believe certain things without investigation or observation. We are convinced to follow the leader. And we will discard truths to hold on to perceptions. We essentially uphold the formality of the story we have been presented instead of the truth we see. We will essentially believe the institutionalization and refuse reality, the formality over the truth. Our own beliefs, our experiences and our casual indoctrination into a culture of separation, cloud our understanding for formality instead of truth.

Knowing the difference between formality and truth is essential to understand politics. Politics is everywhere. Those averse to politics are averse to considering life, because all human life is influenced by politics, politics shapes everything including our perception of formality and truth. Politics, perhaps because of the sheer numbers of those averse to it, shapes individuals more than individuals shape politics. Being able to understand politics is being able to understand humanity, society and progression of that thing we call culture.

The understanding between formality and truth might itself be a measure of mental adulthood as well. The more one obfuscates truth and revels in formality the more infantile or juvenile one likely is. Those who accept formality more than truth normally have some selfish reason to shed truth. Examples of this can be seen in the operation of most any institution where one forgoes the real, for the presented deal. An extreme example of this is the divine right of kings of Europe and Japan, but any leniency to institutions in such a way is giving in to formality and shedding truth. The Citizen's United Supreme Court decision is another example where for all extents and purposes the truth of individual rights is shed in favor for the formality of institutions. You can apply all the formality in the world and convince most everybody in the world that corporation and institutions are people or should have the rights of people, but the fact is institutions are not individuals.

There is barely rarely truth in formality and truth never ever requires formality. Human history is a at its basis story of individuals and institutions and their interplay. History itself is a history of politics. In viewing humankind with historical context one can see this external interplay, one dependent on the other for development. Human history internally is also a history of the mind. Hegel explored this concept in what has become known as the Master - Slave Dialectic.

The idea on one level correlates the development of the human mind with development of human politics from the ancient Egyptians all the way to the European monarchies. Hegel related the external history of mankind with the internal development of the individuals. Two individuals meet, one enslaves the other. Hegel noted that consciousness of the collective or the individual is instigated by the slave, the truth, refusing to obey the master, the formality. Hegel's recital of the history of the revolution of consciousness stopped when he died. But if he could observe history as we do ants and lived longer he would have seen the American Revolution and ensuing Bill of Rights, especially the First Amendment, as one of the higher revolutions of consciousness. The Bill of Rights and the many other constitutional arrangements it inspired was perhaps the ultimate result of the slave defeating the master and since then institutions have infiltrated the revolution to benefit themselves. And the institutions are just the walls of and for certain people to keep out and keep in.

Only brotherhood has allowed man to build and invent and prosper. If it were not for individual brotherhood people would be clamoring for warmth, battling over bones in a constant state of war with perceived outsiders, building deeper and deeper into whatever cavern we occupied building higher and higher walls. The more open one is the more sense of brotherhood one might have. One might feel brotherhood for all, some, a few, or just one person or groups of people. When we realize we are all brothers we don't need walls. When we realize we are all brothers we don't want to hurt each other and feed off of each other.

The fact that our main initiative is to build aboveground and not dig holes so as to have safe hideout for total combat suggests that mankind can be compared to creatures other than antkind. The individuals and institutions that find it necessary to build deeper and deeper caves, with higher and higher walls in more secured institutions are usually the most insect like, the most sadistic and least kind to their fellow man.

The energy corporations and institutions of the world are perhaps the most antlike, gobbling up resources, digging and mining to extract uranium, oil and gas. The time, energy and resources that have been invested into the infrastructure of the petrolithic era and nuclear experimentation is incalculable. The netherworld industries are based on inhuman lies and practices which void consideration of clean air, clean water and healthy food. Where humanity would be today without nuclear experimentation is impossible to say, but without it, surely the planet would be less toxic and polluted. I submit that, simply because necessity is mother of invention, if it were not for nuclear experimentation humanity could already have free, or for all extents and purposes endless and harmless, power sources. Because we have nuclear power, because we have been induced to believe it is modern technology and not totally experimental and deadly, there has not been the impetus for the last sixty seven plus years to search out less deadly energy sources. Moreover, because of the oligarchical collectivism exhibited in the nuclear experimentation industry, from the subsidization of the Price Anderson Act onward, it's not so wild to suggest that energy alternatives are suppressed, since the subsidization of nuclear experimentation necessarily also acts to suppress more desirable alternatives, even potentially unscrupulously.

Conspiracies related to the suppression of solar power and quelling electric vehicles are well known. There are also ocean currents, not far offshore of the East Coast which have been turning for the last couple thousand years or so and could spin underwater turbines to generate enormous amounts of power, without dangerous repercussions. This power facility would indeed be 'too cheap to meter', a slogan from the early days of nuclear power experimentation. Harnessing energy from ocean currents is just scratching the surface of 'alternative' power. But why bother when you got nuclear power? Wind, wave, solar and water power sources belittle nuclear experimentation, for they are safe and endless. Any source of power is better than nuclear experimentation, however none is as oligarchical.

The dangers of nuclear experimentation have always been belittled, while the benefits of nuclear experimentation have always been exaggerated. It is an industry of truth omission and information exaggeration. It is the industry which most frequently states "there is no immediate danger to the public" and it is the one which most frequently lies about the public dangers it poses, to all life on Earth.

When it comes to any subject, especially one as dynamic as nuclear experimentation, there are things we know and things we don't know. There are four types of information, as elaborated on by the likes of Socrates and hinted at by Donald Rumsfeld. And as empirically obvious, the more dynamic and serious the subject the more likely people will ignore all information pertaining to it. The subject of global environmental destruction is such an extreme subject, ignored to the point society continues to argue over humanity's effects on temperature rather than change our toxic ways, with no reasoning but oligarchical rewards.

The four types of information are the known knowns and the unknown unknowns. There are also known unknowns and finally, unknown knowns. The fourth part is the most difficult to quantify; these are intuitive or instinctual insights within self and secret held by others. Donald didn't mention this fourth part, for he likely operated entirely through secrets and the unknown knowns.

The knowns of nuclear experimentation and its negative consequences to life, it's economic and societal costs, is enough to demand we cease it everywhere. And what of the unknown unknowns? What implications for the Earth does promotion of global nuclear experimentation have of which we are ignorant? What unknown knowns does the nuclear experimentation industry possess that they are not sharing?

One interesting known known is that the nuclear industry all over the world lies and omits the truth for each other revealed in the EPA turning off public access to radiation detection equipment on the west coast after the Fukushima meltdowns. It is known that, Japan and TEPCO, refused to admit there was any danger to the public, before disclosing there was an accident, then admitting there were partial meltdowns, later that there were meltdowns and ultimately admitting that multiple complete meltthroughs had occurred.

The safety of nuclear experimentation has always been a subject the institutionalized have lied about and the dangers associated with it have never been and could never be exaggerated. It is obvious that the nuclear experimentation claw of the Wendigo world has directly and indirectly eliminated alternative power systems to the extraction of and concoction of dangerous minerals through its diabolical influence and outright subversion of systems less oligarchical.

The claw of the Wendigo can be countered with the hand of man and the five stages of revolution as depicted in The First Amendment. We have to take off the falsehoods we built around us and others ceremoniously like antkind. We have to come out from underground or under the figurative institutional configurations which keep us separated. We have to remove ourselves from under institutions and become unstitutional and pro individual.

Which came first, war or walls? We need to stop building literal and mental walls, so we would be one ant colony, so as to eliminate the bordermind. We can thank god the creator or Earth Mother for the fact that ants incessantly war on each other. If ants didn't war on each other they would have likely taken over the world, Earth would be theirs. The controlling institutions are the same, they are thankful individuals will still war so they can control, if we did not insist on the forceful self-destructive war state, we could begin to move forward past the netherworld oligarchy.

"Treat the Earth well. It was not given to you by your parents. It was loaned to you by your children." ~Indian Proverb

Please consider leaving a review for The Little Green Revolution and check out Ethan Indigo's other books like 108 Steps to Be in The Zone, The Matrix of Four, Santa Clause Syndrome and the Terraist Letters.

48692880R00082

Made in the USA
Middletown, DE
25 September 2017